James Nash: A Tribute

Environmental Ethics, Ecumenical Engagement, Public Theology

James Nash: A Tribute
Environmental Ethics,
Ecumenical Engagement, Public Theology

edited by
Norman Faramelli & Rodney L. Petersen

BOSTON THEOLOGICAL INSTITUTE

NEWTON CENTRE, MA 02459

James Nash: A Tribute, Environmental Ethics, Ecumenical Engagement, Public Theology
Norman Faramelli, Rodney L. Petersen, editors

First Paperback Edition 2010

 BOSTON THEOLOGICAL INSTITUTE
ISBN 978-0-9843796-0-6

Cover design & artwork: Marian Gh. Simion

© 2010 Boston Theological Institute
210 Herrick Road, Sturtevant Hall
Newton Centre, MA 02459

21st Century Ministry Booklets ISSN: 1940-7866
Marian Gh. Simion, *Managing Editor*

ISBN 978-0-9843796-0-6

Printed in the United States of America by Arvest Press, Inc., Waltham, MA.

James A. Nash

dedicated

to Millie
to Noreen and Rebecca
and to Haley

Table of Contents

Foreword:
James A. Nash and the Wider Ecumenical Movement

By Rodney L. Petersen

Jim Nash's work on environmental ethics, its relation to ecumenical engagement and to public theology, grows out of a context of increasing concern for the world, its ecological integrity and the well being of all sentient life. These are not topics easily objectified. As the theologian Jürgen Moltmann reminds us, "What we call the environmental crisis is not merely a crisis in the natural environment of human beings. It is nothing less than a crisis in human beings themselves." James Nash was aware of this and it drove him to write not only about nature and the human predicament but also about related topics in public theology with relation to church and society.

Ecumenical Engagement

Nash's ecumenical engagement was related to the justice and peace concerns of the World Council of Churches (WCC), framed at its Vancouver General Assembly in 1983. The emerging conceptual framework, "Justice, Peace, and the Integrity of Creation," itself was grounded in thinking that extends back to the Conference on Church and Society (Geneva, 1966), which had the theme "Christians in the Technical and Social Revolutions of our Time." These concerns frame Nash's work with councils of churches, the Churches' Center for Theology and Public Policy in Washington, D. C., and in his teaching.

The Fourth Assembly of the WCC (Uppsala, Sweden, 1968) had urged further work in this area at a time when many physical and social scientists were beginning to alert the human community of the danger of resource depletion and environmental collapse. A series of Working Committees on Church and Society in the early 1970's began to link concern for social justice with an awareness of growing ecological problems. The conference "Science and Technology for Human Development: An Ambiguous Future – and Christian

Hope," held in Bucharest, Romania (1974), was a result of this thinking. The Fifth Assembly of the WCC (Nairobi, Kenya, 1975) received this work and, stimulated by the able thinking of the Australian biologist Charles Birch, adopted through its Central Committee in the following year, the program area "The Struggle for the Just, Participatory and Sustainable Society." The Committee authorized work for a conference in 1979 which was eventually held at the Massachusetts Institute of Technology (MIT), occurring during Nash's tenure as executive director of the Massachusetts Council of Churches.

Environmental Ethics

In his remarks at the MIT conference "Nature, Humanity and God in Ecological Perspective," Charles Birch laid a foundation for environmental ethics by contending that we have created a mechanistic cosmology of science out of what was once perhaps a useful tool in severing the cord for science and religion from a worldview suffused with superstition and magic, but that this cosmology is now threatening to redefine who we are. Birch argued for a more integrative approach, suffused with subjectivity, in our relations with nature as informed by process theology. Nash's environmental ethics reflect these concerns, the rejection of epistemological dualism, an affirmation of the integration of society and ecosystems, the relation between God and God's creation, solidarity with other religious traditions and deepened science and religion dialogue. Nash took up these concerns in his book *Loving Nature* (1991) and it continued to course through his later work.

The MIT conference continues to stand as a watershed in contemporary ethical environmental thinking. Perhaps the most important insight it raised had to do with the relationship between ecology and worldview, as this one issue helps to shape the conception of so many other issues. We can credit persons like Thomas Berry, Brian Swimme – and Nash – for helping to awaken us to the importance of understanding the contributions of the spiritual and historical stories of all peoples, as partners at a table set by contemporary mechanistic science and the older western Jewish and Christian theologies. What is new since MIT is the way in which the debate over "the integrity of creation" has been drawn into that over Gospel and culture. Nash's article, "Humility as a Predisposition for Sustainability," is an appropriate dialogue partner here.

Public Theology

Nash was concerned with the question of worldview and how it understood and portrays its grounding in Christian theology concerning biotic and natural rights. Whether nature is best understood in mechanistic terms or is symbolic of a deeper mystery is a question at the core of theology in this century. Indeed no less a (socio-)biologist than E. O. Wilson reminds us of the stakes involved in how we answer this question when he writes, "The great philosophical divide in moral reasoning about the remainder of life is whether or not other species have an innate right to exist. The decision rests in turn on the most fundamental question of all, whether moral values exist apart from humanity, in the same manner as mathematical laws, or whether they are idiosyncratic constructs that evolved in the human mind through natural selection, and thus of the spirit."

This question, central to contemporary theology, animates Nash's public theology in such a way as to reflect his grounding in the life of the churches and their ecumenical and inter-faith congregational realities.

Congregations of faith, asked to discuss the use of Styrofoam cups in church functions, are led to inquire about their most fundamental life assumptions. Debate over the endangered spotted owl leads persons to reflection with other religious traditions about world views. Decisions which need to be made concerning pollution in local drinking water or toxic waste drive communities to reflect on issues of ecological justice and the premises from which they are derived – something Nash did frequently as in his article, "On the Subversive Virtue: Frugality" (1997), as a way to break inordinate dependence on intensive production and consumption. The environmental crisis for Nash was not just about ecology. It mirrors the understanding and attitudes that we have about ourselves. It reminds us that our "inner ecology" helps to define and give shape to the "outer ecology."

Introduction

By Norman Faramelli

On April 21, 2010 the Ethics Group of the Boston Theological Institute (in conjunction with the Massachusetts Council of Churches) held a Tribute to James Nash celebrating his contributions to environmental ethics, ecumenical engagement and political theology. Jim Nash died in November 2008 and the Ethics group was particularly saddened, since he was an active participant and creative colleague at BTI until the last stages of his illness. Since Jim Nash also spent 21 years on the staff at the Massachusetts Council of Churches (including 13 years as Executive Director), it was important that this event was planned with the Mass Council.

The purpose of the event was not only to celebrate Jim's contributions but also to show how his work has influenced and continues to influence many in the field of environmental ethics. A similar tribute to Nash and his work was held at the Society of Christian Ethics Annual Meeting (in San Jose, CA, January 2010), where Nash had been an active participant for many years.

I had the opportunity to assemble a panel of ethicists, theologians, doctoral students and Church leaders for this occasion, and also serve as the moderator. The panelists were from various Christian denominations- Episcopal, Roman Catholic, Methodist, Lutheran, United Church of Christ and Baptist. James Nash was widely known as a first rate environmental ethicist – both nationally and internationally. Less known, however, were his many contributions to the ecumenical movement, the ecumenical spirit, and to ecumenical theology and ethics.

In my introductory remarks, I focused exclusively on Jim's work with the Massachusetts Council of Churches and his manifold contributions to the ecumenical movement, as well as my long time association with him. My remarks are summarized in the first part of the Background Paper written in preparation for the April 21 event.

After the introductory remarks, H. Paul Santmire, widely respected Lutheran theologian and also one of the pioneers in the theology of ecology, spoke of Nash's amazing theological achievements in a very difficult environment. Santmire noted how Nash "did the theologically improbable and allegedly theological impossible in a theologically accessible way."

John Hart, Roman Catholic ethicist and Professor at Boston University, addressed "Love and Rights on Common Ground." Hart spoke appreciatively on how the love of nature and the emphasis on biotic rights in Nash's work is in sync with the views of certain native Americans (Phillip Deere).

There were three consecutive presentations by doctoral students from the Boston University School of Theology, all of whom are Methodists. Two of them had been students of Nash (Grenfell-Lee and Marcum) and the third doctoral student (Mawokomatanda) while not studying with Nash, was deeply influenced by his writings.

Marla Marcum spoke of Nash's influence on her work in environmental ethics, especially her politically active work in climate change. She particularly emphasized how Nash influenced her understanding of action and reflection, a style that Nash himself embodied. Shandirai Mawokomatanda spoke on how Nash's understanding of biotic rights and political ecology can be helpful in addressing the ecological conditions in his homeland, Zimbabwe. Tallessyn Grenfell-Lee spoke not only of Nash's impact on her as a mentor but also on how his work has widened her visions of ecofeminism.

James Antal, Senior Minister of the Massachusetts United Church of Christ (largest Protestant denomination in Massachusetts) spoke of the need for the Church to address ecological issues, especially the threats resulting from global warming. Antal envisioned the Church in the role of a "canary in the coal mine" – an early warning system – to alert people to the dangers of environmental degradation and also to explore and develop positive solutions.

In a concluding socio-cultural observation, Harvard theologian Harvey Cox (also a Baptist minister), gave his positive assessment of Nash's work. Having read "Loving Nature" around the time he saw the James Cameron movie, "Avatar," Cox was struck by the sharp contrast between the artificial view of nature in the movie compared to the realistic view of nature in the work of Nash.

The remarks of the panelists prompted a lively discussion. A brief summary of the comments engendered by the presentations can be found in the last section of this volume.

Background Paper: A Tribute to James A. Nash

By Norm Faramelli

Introduction

This Background Paper is designed to give those who knew Nash Nash and those who did not some overall insights into his career, his ideas, and the progression of those ideas. A biographical sketch (Appendix I) is provided at the end of this paper which deals with Nash's personal life, his experiences growing up in the Pittsburgh area, and other aspects of his life not covered in this text. Although Nash is widely and rightly acclaimed as an environmental ethicist and environmental theologian, his career began in political science, political ethics and ecumenical relations.

This paper begins with Nash's decision to attend seminary and become a minister and traces how his career was shaped. It will also focus on how and why Nash moved into ecumenical work and then into the field of ecological ethics and ecological theology

The Early Boston University Days

In an autobiographical sketch, Nash noted that once he decided to attend seminary, there was no doubt that he would go to Boston University (BU), which he referred to as "the New Jerusalem," because of its work in philosophical theology, the empirical sciences and the Social Gospel tradition.[1]

In 1963, Nash graduated *magna cum laude*. Due to his excellent work, he had expected to graduate in two years, but was informed by Dean Walter Muelder that no one could get through BU in two years. Nash was, however, encouraged by Dean Muelder and Professor Paul Deats to pursue doctoral studies in Social Ethics. In the BU tradition, it was customary for the doctoral students in Social Ethics to work in an interdisciplinary manner and to study a discipline other than Theology and Ethics at a secular institution. Nash chose to go to the London School of Economics and Political Science to study politics and ethics. At the London School, Nash was deeply impressed with the work of Professor Morris Ginsberg, noted British sociologist and moral philosopher and Professor Bernard Crick, who became a prominent political philosopher. Even in the last stages of his life, Nash frequently referred to Professor Crick's influence. While at the London School, Nash became interested in British politics and especially the parliamentary debates. Through his MP, Margaret Thatcher, at that time an unknown politician, Nash got tickets to attend the debates.[2] Nash was always excited about political discourse and dialogue, an interest and skill that remained with him all of his life.

When he began his doctoral studies at BU in Social Ethics with a specialty in political ethics, he could not resist dabbling in ecumenical issues and ecumenical studies. He had a strong interest in political activity and in the role of religious institutions in the political realm. He was also deeply concerned with ecumenical activity and with what helped and what hindered ecumenical action and Church unity. One of the papers he wrote as a doctoral student at BU was "Theological Foundations of Social Thought and Action of the World Council of Churches" (1965).[3] In reading that paper one soon discovers the theological depth of Nash and his profound interest in ecclesiology as well as ethics. Nash's doctoral dissertation at BU was entitled, "Church Lobbying in Federal Government: A Comparative Study of Four Church Agencies in Washington." That dissertation reflected his concerns for politics, social and political advocacy, ecclesiology and ecumenical activity.[4]

The Massachusetts Council of Churches Days

Upon receiving his doctorate, Nash had fully expected to go into teaching, utilizing the Ph.D. that he had long sought. That was not to be, at least for many years.   In 1967, a job opened up at the Massachusetts Council of Churches as Director of Social Relations, a position that resonated with many of Nash's interests and skills. After consultation with Dean Muelder and Professor Deats, both of whom said that might be a good position "for a few years," Nash was hired by the Massachusetts Council of Churches. The "few years" however, turned into twenty-one years! While he was at the Massachusetts Council, I had the opportunity to work with him on issues related to opposition to the Vietnam War, abolition of capital punishment, fair taxation (including the graduated income tax), civil rights, and many others. Nash was also intensely involved in Church-State issues, abortion rights, welfare rights and many other pressing issues.

During Nash's early years at the Council, there was a high turnover of the Executive Directors. In fact, there were two Directors in a period of six years. Both Directors were deeply concerned about the Church's involvement in social action, but they were not primarily concerned with issues of Church unity. During that time, the organization was also plagued with financial woes. After the second Executive Director resigned, Nash was selected to replace him in 1975 because (a) he was competent and the people knew his work (especially in social concerns), (b) he understood Church politics and knew and was trusted by the religious leadership and (c) he had a deep interest in ecumenical activity and Church Unity as well as social and political advocacy.[5]

Nash remained at the Massachusetts Council for thirteen more years as Executive Director and left in 1988. During his tenure as Executive Director, the Council thrived. Under his leadership there was a strong promotion of Church unity and social advocacy. He worked ecumenically with Roman Catholics, Eastern Orthodox and Evangelicals who were not members of the Council. He also initiated interfaith dialogue with the Jewish communities. In this position Nash honed his political and diplomatic skills, and became as some have said "a master of dialogue." Nash prided himself on his ability to get Church leaders to work with and trust each other. In addition, during those thirteen years there was substantial work in social advocacy, and the Massachusetts Council produced and adopted twenty major social policy statements.[6]

One of Nash's favorite Massachusetts Council products was a document entitled: *Odyssey Toward Unity: Foundations and Functions of Ecumenism and Conciliarism* of which Nash was the principal author. The document focused on "the marks of a truly ecumenical body." He wrote that:

A council of churches which is a truly ecumenical body is defined… as one which intentionally attempts to function as a forerunner of Greater Church unity and which seeks to fulfill in programs and activities the fundamental purposes of the Church which the member-bodies hold in common.

Five of the marks of a truly ecumenical body are shared worship, dialogue, ecumenical advocacy, evangelism and social mission.[7]

This document was not only utilized in Massachusetts, but was widely recognized by Councils of Churches throughout the nation as a useful guide. Avery Post, a former executive of the Massachusetts Conference of the United Church of Christ and later the denomination's president, noted, "It seems to me that you…have begun to strike the pace for which you are seeking over the years. It is a quality product—a leadership statement."[8]

Nash loved to engage in dialogue and he always was intensely interested in the stuff of politics. He died the day after Barack Obama won the presidential election, and he was not content just to know that Obama had won. Nash wanted to have a state-by-state breakdown of the voting results (probably, the political junkie in him, wanted to study the results to see if the Obama victory was fluke or was a harbinger of new things to come).

Nash's ecumenical leadership was widely recognized across the nation. In 1981, he was chosen to chair the National Workshop on Church Unity. The prior year, he wrote an insightful article on the Church in and beyond politics. Nash was always deeply sensitive to the need for balance. There are pitfalls of ignoring politics, on the one hand, and the dangers of going in 'head over heels' into political action, on the other. According to Nash, the standard for evaluating Churches should be as follows: "A Church not in politics has lost its mission, but a Church which is not beyond politics has lost its prophetic commission."[9]

One of the last articles Nash wrote as an ecumenical leader appeared in the *Journal of Ecumenical Studies* entitled, "Political Conditions for Ecumenical Confession-Protestant Contributions to Ecumenical Dialogue." Nash realized that some of the Protestant denominations were having difficulty with the Nicene Creed, and he spelled out five political conditions that needed to be met in order to address the issues. For example, he wrote that the *'filioque'* clause in the Nicene Creed should be discarded, not just on doctrinal grounds but on ethical grounds. That is, the Western Church had no right to insert it into the Nicene Creed without the consent of the Eastern Church. Nash also noted that the reader should not fret about political conditions, because the Council of Nicaea and other Church Councils were filled with politics and political solutions, something that often gets ignored when we plunge into the theological details.[10]

Bird Watching, Eco-Justice and the Move to Washington

Nash was an avid birder and hiker throughout his life – and he took bird watching very seriously not just as a form of recreation. His ability to offer a discourse on the origins and habits of each species was remarkable, and he could do that while enjoying the birds in flight. It was in birding that he developed his passionate love of nature.

In the early 1970's Nash became interested in a program we at the Boston Industrial Mission were developing for national denominations in Eco-Justice. It was clear that in this program Nash was able to combine his political interests, love of nature, ecology, and his passion for social justice and social policy. Nash helped us organize a series of sessions throughout the Commonwealth of Massachusetts in various Churches of different denominations in order to communicate the eco-justice message. Despite his own personal interests, eco-justice did not become a priority of the Council in the late 1970s and 1980s.

When Nash left the Council of Churches, he went to head up the Churches' Center for Theology and Public Policy in Washington, D. C. At that time, he also began teaching as Wesley Theological Seminary. It was during the late 80's through his work at the Center and through his teaching at Wesley that Nash honed his skills as an environmental/ecological ethicist, resulting in the publication of *Loving Nature: Ecological Integrity and Christian Responsibility*.[11]

James Nash: The Environmental/Ecological Ethicist and Theologian

Loving Nature
Loving Nature was indeed a pioneering work, and it is still a classic in the field. In this work Nash blended all of his major interests–love of nature, immersion in the empirical sciences, theological reflection, ethical analysis and social and political policy. In this work one can find Nash's profound eco-justice concerns. Despite his deep love of the natural order, he refused to romanticize nature. There are cruelties in nature that need to be respected. Nash began this book with an autobiographical sketch, and laid out the basic ecological problems forcefully and clearly. He then offered a critique of the thesis by Lynn White, Jr., that blamed Christianity for the ecological crisis, which Nash always regarded as an oversimplification of history. Unlike some deep ecologists, Nash fully recognized that humans have been entrusted with specific responsibilities. Nevertheless, it was absolutely necessary for us to move away from an anthropocentric view of the world.[12]

If there is to be a solid Christian ecological ethic it must be based on firm theological foundations. Nash devoted two chapters in *Loving Nature* to Firm Foundations, utilizing the Christian doctrines of Creation, Covenant, Divine Image, Incarnation, Spiritual Presence, Sin, Judgment, Redemption and the Church. Nash was not only an excellent ethicist but a serious theologian as well. When he addressed the motif of *Loving Nature* he understood Christian love in an ecological context, and Love as Ecological Justice with its Rights and Responsibilities. It is here where Nash introduced his understanding of biotic rights along side of human rights.

The last chapter of *Loving Nature* on, "Political Directions for Ecological Integrity," is a synthesis of Nash's interests in politics, public policy, empirical science and social ethics. Nash spoke of the need for sufficient government regulations, our responsibilities to future generations, our guardianship of biodiversity, the need for international cooperation and ecological security and the links between justice, peace and ecology.[13] That was indeed a tall order, and Nash did it well.

Other Writings in Ecological Ethics
In addition to his book, Nash wrote numerous articles on ecology and eco-justice and also lectured widely. Only a few articles are noted here, but some

others are referenced in Appendix II. In an article in 1996 on the "Politician's Moral Dilemma..," Nash confronted the political realities faced by elected officials as he discussed the possibilities and the limits of political leadership in confronting the Ecological Crisis. This article is a review of the book by Al Gore, *Earth in the Balance*, which Nash at first disliked but later gained an appreciation for it and for the political complexities that Gore was addressing.[14]

In a lecture delivered at Virginia Theological Seminary in 1997, Nash called for a new ecological order, which include two basic values – a new virtue, "sustainability" combined with the old virtue of "frugality."[15] (More will be said about frugality when the "Frugality Project" is discussed below.)

In the 1999 Ian Barbour Lecture, Nash called for the virtue of "humility" as a predisposition for sustainability.[16] If we are to address sustainability seriously, then we will need to recognize the limitations (both internal and external) on all human powers. Moreover, we will need to act in accordance with those limitations. In this lecture Nash distinguished between the wider concepts of "sustainability" and the more familiar slogan "sustainable development." If we are to deal with sustainability, then we need to constrain the sovereign rights of nations to exploit their resources, we will need to overcome our anthropocentrism, and will need to shed our simplistic understanding of sustainable material economic growth. Nash fully recognized that his views demanded radical restructuring of the global political economy, and his political understanding never allowed him to underestimate the difficulty of that task.

In an article in the *Encyclopedia of Religion and Nature*,[17] Nash wrote about five fundamental facts in ecology that have to be the features of Christian Ecological Reformation. These are based on an engagement between religion and the biological and ecological sciences. These are: (a) Evolutionary Fecundity – that amazing natural order, with its rich array of species and biota; (b) Biological Kinship – "Humans are linked in biological solidarity with all other forms of life through our common beginnings in one or more living cells and through our subsequent adaptive interactions."(c) Universal Relationality – "Everything is connected with and has consequences for everything else." Being is being in interdependent relationships: as seen in the integration of social justice and ecological reformation – "eco-justice." (d) Biophysical Boundaries – "The planet is finite, essentially self-contained sphere, except for solar energy.... There are no infinite bounties, no inexhaustible resources, no limitless systems." (e) Human Dominance – Humans exercise dominion, a fact that needs to be faced. "The concept of dominion recognizes a basic biological fact; humans alone have evolved the necessary rational and moral capacities, and therefore, the creative and/or destructive powers to represent divine blessings or demonic curses to the rest of the planet's biota." Here Nash takes on those who would minimize human dominion. As noted, it is fact of life, and that is why ecological responsibility (or bio-responsibility) is so necessary.

One on my favorite articles by Nash is his response to his friend Thomas Derr, for years a severe critic of the ecology movement. In an article entitled "In Flagrant Dissent," Nash did what he always did best, engage in serious dialogue with a person holding opposite views.[18] He challenged Derr in seven areas–Stewardship, Theological Foundations, Intrinsic Value, Biotic Rights, Ecofeminism, Environmental Policies as well as the Social Consequences of Biocentrism. Nash flatly rejected the notion of stewardship being limited to managing nature only for human sustainability. He challenged Derr's theology, which did not give sufficient importance to the doctrines of creation, incarnation, the sacramental presence of the Spirit and the hope for cosmic redemption. Nash admitted that Deer was correct in assuming that "intrinsic value" is a threat to his anthropocentric views. In his defense of Biotic Rights, Nash argued that there has to be more than one basis for moral rights–not only the human right of universal equality. "Biotic rights are an effort to redefine responsible human relationships with the rest of the planet's beleaguered biota, and to ground these responsibilities not simply in human generosity and utility but in moral claims inherent in their conation for appropriate treatment."[19] Nash challenged Derr's claim that Ecofeminism is a distraction. Nash fully recognized that patriarchy and anthropocentrism go together hand in glove. Nash challenged Derr's underestimating the nature of ecological problems such as climate change. He also challenged his reliance on conservative political theorists. Nash also challenged Derr's reliance upon the free market to solve ecological problems. Nash also believed that Derr had grossly overestimated the damage resulting from biocentrism, and here he responded with: "Most of us who have described our thought as biocentric or as having biocentric elements, we have tried, in different ways and with different results, to integrate anthropic, biotic and ecosystemic values into our social and ecological ethics, without jeopardizing our commitments to the human project."[20] Nash concluded his response with:

The environmental cause … challenges us to follow a new course–a course that lives within the bounds of nature's regenerative, absorptive and carrying capacities; one that adapts prudently to interdependence of humans with all other planetary elements and processes and one that responds benevolently and justly to the fact of human kinship with all otherkind.[21]

Natural Law, Natural Rights and Biotic Rights
Although Nash was critical of some of the uses of Natural Law, he maintained that some version was necessary in order to do social ethics in a

pluralistic context. He saw some essential elements of natural law in ecological ethics as an affirmation of objective moral values and norms, which correspond to the conditions for flourishing among relational beings. This includes a rational experiential method for evaluation and justifying moral standards, and a dependence on and dialogue with empirical disciplines in searching for "moral norms." It also entails a quest for common moral ground accessible in principle to all humanity and a necessary autonomy from and yet compatibility with basic Christian affirmation of faith.

Nash was, however, deeply concerned that various expressions of the natural law tradition were anthropocentric and had nothing to do with ecological relatedness. That is, much of the natural law tradition simply ignored the physical and biological non-human order. Nash called for a universal and immanent moral order, where the words 'law' and 'nature' are distinguished (i.e., law in the sense of moral norms and obligations) natural (moral values should reflect the reality of human conditions and the planet's whole biota). These norms could be developed through natural reasoning capacities, without relying upon special revelation, but always utilizing the knowledge gained from the empirical sciences. For example, he called for an ecosystemic compatibility—adapting ecologically to natural cycles and constraints and respecting ecosystemic values, an ecologically sensitive theology, the trans-valuing of value, the extension of covenant justice to include all other life forms as beloved creatures, i.e., bioresponsibility, and also reforming our virtues of sustainability and frugality. Seeking moral norms in natural law was spelled out clearly in his article in the Hessel/Ruether volume.[22] Nash spelled the natural rights aspects out further in a paper presented at the Society of Christian Ethics in 1994 on Biotic Rights.[23]

As noted above, the moral claims for biotic rights and human rights are not the same. Nash called for a conative distinction between them. But it is clear that he saw the intrinsic value of the non-human world in a manner where the species have their own inherent (or intrinsic) value independent to their instrumental value to humans.[24]

The Sustainability Dialogue

From 1998 to 2006, Nash convened the Ethics and Sustainability Dialogue Group, a series of off-the-record exchanges between environmental ethicists and representatives from the chlorine chemical industry. He was not only the initiator but also the leader who kept the dialogue going, especially during some stormy sessions. During this time period, several ethicists left the group because of other commitments. One, in particular, noted that he wanted to proclaim not dialogue. But Nash's idea was that to be interdisciplinary we must understand their institutions and values of the industry as well as how ethics can best be articulated in that context. Major parts of the meetings were spent on reviewing technical data, such as the industry's programs for reducing dioxin emissions and improving drinking water quality. These issues were always placed in a wider ecological context by the ethicists.

During the discussions, the issue of sustainability surfaced repeatedly. But it was not just how the chlorine chemical industry could engage in sustainable development but how we could expand the discussion to go beyond sustainable development to deal with the wider issue of sustainability of the planet. Due to changes in staff and resource availability, the dialogue was terminated after a seven and one half-year period. Some were surprised that it lasted for seven and one half years. Other were surprised that it began at all. But its inception and continuation were the result of Nash's leadership and dialogue skills.

It was during this time (2002) that Nash produced an excellent document on "The Character and Conditions of Dialogue; A Realist's Aspirations."[25] Nash defined "dialogue as an interpersonal process of communication between two or more equal parties with strong commitments and divergent perspectives on given issues, for the purpose of mutual enlightenment and transformation." Dialogue is not public debate, it does not entail mediation or conciliation, it is definitely not arbitration and it does not need a product to make it worthwhile. Dialogue allows us to communicate more effectively, learn the skills of listening, share perspectives, see more clearly the complexity and ambiguity, challenges perspectives, etc.

Dialogue is genuine only when parties regard each other as peers and show respect toward each other. Conversion of the other is not the appropriate goal of dialogue. Dialogue thrives only in a safe house or safe harbor. Dialogue does not, however, preclude public advocacy or other actions. Dialogue depends on fidelity to the rules of rational discourse. Nash concluded noting that although dialogue is no panacea, "it is still a powerful tool for dealing with our differences." Nash put these ideas to work very effectively in his seven and one half-year commitment to the Ethics and Sustainability project.

The Later Days at Boston University

Nash returned to Boston in 1998. In 1999, he began teaching at his alma mater Boston University (until 2004) which was a fitting way for him to end a distinguished career. At BU, he taught courses in social, ecological and political ethics and theologies of dialogue. He taught doctoral courses and also introductory courses to Christian Ethics. (In addition to teaching, Nash also served as the convener of the Sustainability Dialogue noted above.) Nash was a remarkable teacher who had the capacity to excite and energize his students.

This excitement will become evident when his former students present at the February 10 celebration.

Nash always had a deep gratitude for the influences of BU on his work and teaching. At a Boston Theological Institute event in 2006 celebrating the work of Walter Muelder, Nash commented with deep appreciation on the extent of that influence. Nevertheless, he also recognized the limitations of Boston Personalism in dealing with environmental ethics and the ecological crisis.[26]

The Frugality Project

The virtue of 'frugality' was always of special interest to Nash. Although 'frugality' was referred to earlier, it deserves a special note. In fact, Nash was commissioned to write a book on that virtue, but due to his illness was never able to complete it. He completed the first chapter on ethical method where he noted that moral philosophers and ethicists are often too rigid in setting boundaries between the various ethical approaches such as deontological, teleological ethics, utilitarianism, and virtue ethics. He was also exploring the work of Thorstein Veblen, going beyond *The Theory of the Leisure Class.*

Nash's major work on 'frugality' was spelled out in a paper published in the *Annual of the Society of Christian Ethics,* a paper presented at a previous annual conference.[27] Nash was a political and economic realist. He understood that 'frugality' is truly a subversive virtue, subversive not just to our ethical system but to the way the entire political economy-based on endless consumption- is structured.

At a time when many were assaulting the federal government, Nash wrote an article with the provocative title: "On the Goodness of Government." In this article, Nash urged political progressives to recognize and acknowledge government screw-ups, but he called for a positive role for government. One such role of government is to provide the social and political conditions for the virtue of frugality to be firmly embedded in the normal way of doing things.[28]

Nash's Final Article

During his illness, Nash shared two articles with me. One was on Biodiversity and the Bible and the other constituted reflections on a document produced by the National Council of Churches. The former was published in the *Journal for the Study of Religion, Nature and Culture* as, "The Bible versus Biodiversity: The Case Against Moral Argument from Scripture." The article appeared with several responses from Nash's friends and colleagues.[29] In this article, Nash made a radical case for why the Bible has limited value in moral argumentation. Most of his respondents thought that he carried his case too far, and he was shortchanging the ethical value of the biblical tradition. Nash did, however, call for a dialogue with the Bible. He also found this approach valuable for "making existential decisions of faith and doing theological interpretation."[30] Nash wrote:

The alternative method for Christian ethical evaluation, justification (or not) and prescription that I encourage is *rational reflection on the fullness of human experience, in dialogue with the Bible and the Christian tradition, on the one hand, and cultural wisdom, especially in the relevant sciences and other religious, moral and philosophical traditions, on the other.*[31]

Nash's last article was a major topic in the forum held in his honor at a recent Society of Christian Ethics meeting in San Jose, CA (January 2010). In the discussion, there was a sense that Nash had not sufficiently valued the Bible in moral decision making. But it was clear that Nash was always leery of simplistic movements from the biblical text to social, political, economic and ecological issues.

Concluding Comments

What has been presented above is a brief glimpse and exposure to the life and work of James A. Nash, our esteemed colleague and friend. His contributions to environmental ethics and eco-justice have been manifold. Although Nash is now widely recognized as a major figure in ecological or eco-justice ethics, it is important that we understand the continuity of his thought from his early BU days, his twenty-one years with the Massachusetts Council of Churches, and his later work in political ethics and public policy as well as his teaching at Wesley Theological Seminary and the Boston University School of Theology.

We in the Ethics group of the Boston Theological Institute will always be grateful for Nash's dedication, friendship, contributions, his energetic personality and, above all, for his generosity of spirit. We have been graced by his presence among us and celebrate the time he spent with us.

ENDNOTES
[1] "Autobiographical Sketch." This is an unpublished paper found in the Nash files, with a note by Nash, "written probably for the Faculty Retreat at Wesley Theological Seminar, 1993-1994."
[2] Ibid.
[3] Unpublished paper in Nash files, dated Dec. 4, 1965.
[4] Nash 's dissertation is available at the library of the Boston University School of Theology.
[5] Nordbeck, Elizabeth, *"That They May all be One": Celebrating a Century of Ecumenical Witness* (Boston: Massachusetts Council of Churches, 2002), pp 39-44.
[6] Ibid., p 40.
[7] *Odyssey Toward Unity; Foundations and Functions of Ecumenism and Conciliarism* (Committee on Purpose and Goals of Ecumenism; Boston: Massachusetts Council of Churches, March 1975).

[8] Nordbeck, op. cit. p 41.

[9] Nash, James, "In, Yet Beyond Politics: The Role of Churches in the Affairs of State." Revised Oct. 20, 1980; unpublished found in Nash files. (It was used as a teaching document at the Massachusetts Council.)

[10] Nash, James, "Political Conditions for Ecumenical Confession: A Protestant Contribution to the Emerging Dialogue," *Journal of Ecumenical Studies,* 25:2, Spring 1988 (The '*filioque*' clause – "and the Son" – was added to "proceeded from the Father" in the Nicene Creed by the Western Church in the 7th century.)

[11] Published by Abington Press (Nashville, TN) in cooperation with the Churches Center for Theology and Public Policy, second printing 1992. For an excellent review of the book see Susan Power Bratton in *Environmental Ethics,* spring 1993.

[12] Ibid., See especially chapter 2: "Ecological Complaint Against Christianity," pp 68-92.

[13] Ibid., Ch. 8, pp 182-222.

[14] Nash, James, "The Politician's Moral Dilemma: The Moral Possibilities and Limits of Political Leadership Confronting the Ecological Crisis," *CTNS Bulletin* (Center for Theology and the Natural Sciences), Vol. 16, No. 1 (Winter 1996).

[15] Nash, James, "The Old Order Changeth: The Ecological Challenge to Christian Life and Thought," *Virginia Seminary Journal,* Dec 1997 (1997 Spriggs Lecture).

[16] Nash, James, "Humility as Predisposition for Sustainability," *Bulletin of Science, Technology and Society,* Vol. 19, No. 5 (Oct. 1999).

[17] Nash, James, "Christianity, Contemporary," in the *Encyclopedia of Religion and Nature,* ed. Bron Taylor (2005). Nash also served on the editorial board of the Encyclopedia.

[18] Nash, J.; "In Flagrant Dissent: An Environmentalist Contention," in Thomas Derr, with James Nash and Richard Neuhaus in *Environmental Ethics and Christian Humanism* (Nashville, TN: Abington Press, 1996).

[19] Ibid, p 111.

[20] Ibid., p123.

[21] Ibid., p 124.

[22] See Nash, James, "Seeking Moral Norms in Nature: Natural Law and Ecological Responsibility," in Hessel, Dieter and Ruether, Rosemary Radford, eds.; *Christianity and Ecology: Seeking the Well-Being of the Earth and Humans* (Cambridge, MA: Harvard University Press, 2000), p. 8.

[23] See "Biotic Rights and Human Ecological Responsibility," in *The Annual of the Society of Christian Ethics* (1993) as well as "Case for Biotic Rights," *Yale Journal of International Law,* vol. 1, No. 11 (1993), pp 235-49.

[24] See also the above response to T. Derr.

[25] Unpublished paper that was used in the Sustainability Dialogue and was periodically revised. It was also used in Nash's teaching at Boston University.

[26] Nash, James, "Walter G. Muelder: Boston Personalism Incarnate," in *The Significance of Walter G. Muelder's Social Ethics Today: The Present Status of Personalism* (Newton, MA: Boston theological Institute, 2006).

[27] Nash, James, "Toward the Revival and Reform of the Subversive Virtue: Frugality," *The Annual of the Society of Christian Ethics,* 1995.

[28] *Theology and Public Policy,* Vol VII, No. 2 (Winter 1995), pp 2-25.

[29] *Journal for the Study of Religion, Nature and Culture,* Vol. 3. no. 2 (2009). Responses were written by Carol Robb, Michael Northcott, James Childs, Jr., Ellen Davis, Norm Faramelli, Celia Deane-Drummond, Bernard Daley Zaleha, and Jay McDaniel.

[30] Ibid.

[31] Ibid, p 232. The italics are in the text.

On the Theological Achievement of James A. Nash

H. Paul Santmire

It is a privilege for me to reflect about the theological achievement of James Nash. I will focus on the theology that comes to expression in his still unsurpassed volume, *Loving Nature: Ecological Integrity and Christian Responsibility* (Nashville: Abingdon, 1991). In response to what may well be the defining challenge of our era in human history, the global ecojustice crisis, Jim Nash did the theologically improbable and allegedly the theologically impossible in a theologically accessible way. I want to elaborate now on each of these points, the *improbable*, the *impossible*, and the *accessible*.

First, the *improbable*. In these times of widespread human impoverishment and advanced ecological turmoil, when the Christian churches and their leaders – Catholic, Orthodox, Mainline Protestant, Evangelical, and Ecumenical – have become highly visible advocates of ecojustice and the integrity of the earth, it may be difficult even to imagine the theological situation faced by Jim Nash and others of us, who first addressed the challenge of an "ecological reformation" of Christianity in the sixties, seventies, and eighties of the last century. We knew that something momentous was unfolding in the world around us and we felt called upon to address the then emerging crisis, but we also felt very much alone–and without viable theological resources with which to work.

The theology we had inherited was self-consciously anthropocentric or, in Karl Barth's memorable terminology, "the-anthropocentric." Its chief concern was God and humanity, often to the disinterest in or even to the total abandonment of the wider world of nature. With the exception of only a few theological projects, such as Paul Tillich's or Joseph Sittler's or the then emerging thought of Juergen Moltmann, dogmatic or systematic theology, was the-anthropocentric. Biblical studies, championed by the self-consciously existential New Testament interpretation of Rudolf Bultmann and his followers, and the over-against-nature Old Testament theology of G. Ernest Wright, were also generally the-anthropocentric. Ethics, whether domesticated

in the form of personal, so-called contextual ethics or more public in the form
of the ethics of technology or the ethics of politics, was likewise mainly the-
anthropocentric. The larger world of nature was not considered in its own
right. It was viewed mainly as the stage for human history and the world of
resources given to humans by God for the sake of human well-being.

That Jim Nash should have published such a substantive and holistic
theological ethics that reclaimed the wider world of nature in *that* theological
environment, was indeed improbable. It was also *impossible*, in this ironic
sense. The word out on the secular streets in those decades was that classical
Christian theology was ecologically bankrupt. This was the infamous
"ecological complaint against Christianity" that Jim Nash wrote about with
such insight in *Loving Nature*.

Christianity, it was argued, was thoroughly anthropocentric and
androcentric, patriarchal and hierarchical; it was essentially a faith of men
over against women and nature. It was also a faith, said the critics, that all
too easily found ways to support the powerful old-boys' networks and their
domination of the earth and the poor of the earth. So, according to the critics,
invoking Christian theology to respond to the global crisis would be like trying
to extinguish a fire by throwing kerosine on it.

A number of theologians, strikingly, adopted this kind of critique as their
own. Gordon Kaufman did this explicitly, arguing that classical Christian
theology was irreformably personalistic and therefore anthropocentric and
therefore useless and even dangerous in this, our ecological and nuclear
era. Others, such as John Cobb and process thinkers of a like mind, tended
to accept the ecological complaint against classical Christianity implicitly,
insofar as they sought to provide totally new foundations for their theological
arguments and to build reconstructed doctrines of God and Christ and the
Spirit on those new foundations. Ecofeminist theologians, such as Rosemary
Ruether and Sallie McFague, did much the same. The only viable future for
Christian theology in our ecological era, they all seemed to be saying, was
the way of thoroughgoing reconstruction. Which was to suggest that any
other way, surely any theology which took the classical Christian tradition as
a framework in which to work, was–impossible.

Nor did it help in those decades that many voices of the Church's own
theological establishment–seminary professors, parish pastors, and writers
of popular theology manuals–responded to the ecological complaint against
Christianity with sometimes simplistic repristenations of traditional church
teachings, above all that beloved construct of bourgeois Christianity in North
America, stewardship. While such spokespersons in defense of classical

Christian thought were undoubtedly well-intended, their stewardship message was, indeed, preaching to the choir or rather whistling in the dark.

The theology of stewardship all too easily seemed to reenforce capitalist ideas that nature is essentially a world of resources at the disposal of humans, for the sake of economic development. That stewardship themes were so easily co-opted by the "wise use" doctrines of corporate extraction-industries proved how unstable and, finally, how theologically unreliable those theological themes were in practice. Which trends, when viewed by those who had eyes to see, seemed to put the finishing nail in the coffin of classical Christian theology. If such an often-times dysfunctional doctrine, stewardship, was *all* that Christian theology had to offer, then could there be any doubt that it was and is ecologically bankrupt? Many thoughtful observers, some within, many outside, the walls of our churches would therefore conclude that the very notion of a Christian ecological theology was indeed a contradiction in terms.

In 1991, in the wake of all these trends, Jim Nash demonstrated that a Christian ecological theology, developed within the context of classical Christian thought, although seemingly improbable and allegedly impossible, was in fact possible, and indeed doable with intellectual zest and insight and integrity. He did not trumpet his loyalty to classical Christian traditions defensively. He simply let those traditions speak for themselves, in his own, well-tuned and rich theological voice. So he stated, boldly and uncompromisingly, in *Loving Nature*: "The Christian faith, despite its historical ambiguities in its ecological credentials, has the impressive potential to become an indestructibly firm foundation for ecological integrity. The faith contains all things necessary, all the values and virtues, for ecological integrity." (p.92)

Nash then proceeded impressively to reframe classical Christian thought ecologically. He drew out ecological meanings from the whole range of Christian teachings, not just from creation-theology, but also from teachings about sin, Christ, the church, the Spirit, and eschatology. His subsequent discussions of ecological ethics are as forceful as they are in significant measure because of those comprehensive and therefore firm theological foundations.

A good example of those firm theological foundations is Nash's reflections about a classical theological theme that sounds esoteric to some and that is sometimes treated as obsolete by others—eschatology. Although Nash believes, with St. Paul, that we "see through a glass darkly" in these matters, Nash nevertheless grounds significant ethical affirmations on the theological vision of the consummation of the creation: "Ecologically, this vision gives ultimate meaning and worth to the cosmic ecosphere... Nothing is any longer valueless or meaningless or irrelevant. Every living creature counts for itself and for God ultimately. This perspective stands in judgment on anthropocentrism... Again, the divine purposes are cosmocentric and biocentric, not simply anthropocentric. Christian ethics must take that fact into account in a process of ecologically-conscious reformation." (pp.132f.)

On this basis, Nash then identifies the Christian ethical mandate: "Our moral responsibility, then, is to approximate the harmony of the New Creation to the fullest extent possible under the constricted conditions of the creation." (p.133) Of interest in this connection, is the fact that he only mentions "stewardship" once in *Loving Nature*, and then only in order to distance himself from use of that construct. The idea of stewardship does not do justice to the New Creation ethics that Nash is seeking to develop.

This brings me to my last observation about Nash's theological achievement. It is not only true that he did the improbable and indeed the allegedly impossible. It is also true that he achieved all this in a way that is *accessible*. By this I do not mean to suggest that Nash wrote as a popularizer, although his argumentation is clear and his style is consistently energetic. Rather, I mean to suggest that Nash developed his argument in a way that can be readily grasped by those many churches which themselves continue to honor classical Christian theology as their own.

Contrast this to a range of other theologians who also eagerly have sought to convert the churches to an ecological vision, but who have done so, sometimes, with theological constructions in hand that have appeared to deviate dramatically from classical Christian teachings, for example, denying the Resurrection of Jesus or reducing its import to the merely metaphorical or identifying the created world with the body of God or announcing that eschatology no longer makes any sense. This is not to suggest that such thoughts are not worthy of our attention and serious discussion. It is rather to observe that theologies that embody such thoughts *ipso facto* make themselves less accessible, and sometimes inaccessible, to a broad range of church leaders around the world today. Not so Jim Nash. His was a powerful voice for the ecological reformation of Christianity from *within* the pale of the classical Christian tradition. So, in this sense, Christians in our ecumenical churches today have no excuse not to listen to him and not to take his thought with thoroughgoing seriousness.

Will they listen? Will Jim Nash's *improbable* and allegedly *impossible* theological project, *accessible* as it is to the ecumenical churches, be taken with the seriousness that it deserves in these times of crisis? I would like to think that the impressive commitments to ecojustice and to the integrity of creation on the part of our ecumenical churches that I referred to at the outset are being nurtured, perhaps unconsciously, by the kind of theology that Jim Nash developed in 1991 and thereafter, along with a few other theological forerunners who labored, often in isolation, in those decades. Of this we can be sure, however. Our ecumenical churches will be well-served today, if their theologians and other leaders find a way to revisit and consciously to reclaim the ecologically reframed classical Christian theology that so richly informs Jim Nash's *Loving Nature.*

Love and Rights on Common Ground: James A. Nash's Love of Nature

By John Hart

In his seminal work, *Loving Nature: Ecological Integrity and Christian Responsibility* (1991), James Nash provided a foundation for environmental concern and ecological ethics. This book, and his other writings and social involvement, inspired or guided community activists, academics, pastors, members of congregations, and the public at large from diverse religious traditions. Reflection on two of Nash's insights—that love should characterize human *relationships* with nonhuman biota, and that people should acknowledge and consider the biotic *rights* of otherkind in their life on Earth as they derive their sustenance and livelihood from Earth's natural goods —could help people find common ground not only with each other as they express ecological concern and exercise ecological care, but also common ground with all life on the Earth that is their common context and home, an Earth where all life shares in the sacramental presence of God-immanent.

In *Loving Nature*, James Nash establishes love as the ground of Christian theology and ethics;[1] suggests seven "dimensions of love";[2] proposes seven environmental rights focused on human needs;[3] and offers a "Bill of Biotic Rights" that suggests eight rights for nonhuman species and individuals.[4] In his writings and lectures, Nash described humanity as an integral part of creation, not as a somehow external, superior component of the natural world. As he states in *Loving Nature*, "The intrinsic value or worth of human beings seems to me to be indefensible apart from the intrinsic value or worth of the biophysical world as a whole, of which human beings are descendants and inseparable parts."[5] In these words, he expressed ideas complementary to those of another of my friends, Phillip Deere, a Muskogee (Creek) spiritual leader, human rights activist, and traditional healer. A spiritual thinker much like James Nash, and a periodic Methodist pastor, he declared:[6]

We were told to respect everything within the creation because…the human being is the most dependent being in creation…. But somewhere down through history we made ourselves believe that we are better than everything within the creation, and that we could make things better…. Somewhere down the history of the human race we began to wander away, and we drifted away from those natural ways of thinking to where we no longer think like our ancestors did, and we forget about nature.

We believe in natural laws of love, peace and respect…. When we destroy anything within the creation, we feel that we destroy ourselves…. We have felt ourselves to be a part of the creation: not superiors, not the rulers of the creation…. If we understand the natural ways, [the] natural laws of love, peace and respect…. We will learn to love and share with everyone.

This paper will use James Nash's insights to consider four themes: first, love as the foundation for creation care; second, the immanence of the Creator in creation; third, nonhuman rights; and fourth, nature's natural rights (the latter as a reflective response to Nash's work on these themes).[7]

1. Love: Foundation for Creation Care

James Nash declared that "a Christian ecological ethic is seriously deficient…unless it is grounded in Christian love."[8] He noted that "Christianity affirms that love is the ground and goal of all being. God *is* love…."[9] If God is love, "the process of creation itself is an act of love. All creatures, human and otherkind, and their habitats are not only gifts of love but also products of love and recipients of ongoing love."[10]

As they experience the presence of the Spirit in creation, reflective Christians might realize that Jesus' teaching in the parable of the Good Samaritan has consequences far beyond those ordinarily understood by interpreters:

Our neighbors who are to be loved are all God's beloved creatures. The "love of nature" is simply the "love of neighbor" universalized in recognition of our common origins, mutual dependencies, and shared destiny with the whole creation of the God who is all-embracing love.[11]

Here, then, is a creative, thoughtful, valuable, and value-laden extension of "the neighbor" to include not solely the despised human "other" suffering from violence and neglect, but all creatures, humankind and otherkind. This reinforces such biblical teachings as those exemplified in the first Creation Story, in which God declares that *all* creation and creatures are "very good," and its complementary Flood Story passages in which God affirms this teaching:

at the beginning of the story God instructs Noah to save a reproductive pair of every living creature threatened by the inundation, and at the end of the story God makes a covenant with Earth, humans, and every living creature, free and domesticated. As shall be discussed later, a further development of these seminal ideas might mean, for some in the Christian and other traditions, that, in order to protect creatures from extinction, not only must their intrinsic value be acknowledged; their *natural* rights in nature and before nature's God must also be safeguarded.

2. Creator in Creation

In *Loving Nature*, James Nash states that: "We experience God as love in the mysteries of creation."[12] He describes how the immanence of the Spirit present in and relating to creation is perceptible to the discerning eye:

The biophysical world provides traces of and testimonies to the mystery and majesty of God....The holy (not wholly) transcendent God is also immanent in the creation. The natural is simultaneously preternatural. God exists *in* the creation as the Holy Spirit [and, as] the immanent Spirit, God is intimate with the creation, actively involved, self-revealing, and grace-dispensing, leaving signs and making the divine presence felt in all things—in personal, cultural, and natural histories...Indeed, the primary source of faith and the primary data for theological reflection are...religious experiences mediated through the sensate.[13]

There is, then, a "sacramental presence" of the Creator in creation:

[W]e live in a "sacramental universe," as William Temple eloquently argued, in which the whole of material existence is essentially holy, because it can be an effective medium of revelation and a vehicle of communion with god, a means of grace. The creation is a sacramental expression of the Creator. Since God dwells in the creation...the world is the bearer of the holy, the temple of the Spirit. For the spiritually receptive, therefore, the cosmos is a complex of sacramental signs that convey the hidden but real presence of the Spirit.[14]

Once again, Nash provides seeds for the further growth and flourishing of his thought. To the preceding might be added the understanding that we live not only in a sacramental *universe*: we live, too, in a sacramental *commons*, the local locus of the sacramental universe, the places in which we can experience the Creator (ordinarily mediated by creation), and in which we should share available natural goods (erroneously called "resources," which can tend to mean a benefit waiting to be extracted and modified by humankind), provided by the creating Spirit, with other creatures who need to inhabit shared and sacred space with humanity, and partake of its goods to provide for their own sustenance.

3. Nonhuman Natural Rights

James Nash advocates for human rights in particular, and biotic rights in general. In the latter case, biotic *rights* are related to the intrinsic *value* of nonhuman life. The recognition of other species' intrinsic value, in turn, is related to Christian understandings of God: "Since loyalty to God entails loyalty to God's values, Christians are called to practice biophilia. All life forms have intrinsic value, and are to be treated with appropriate care and concern."[15]

Nash declares, too, that "Moral rights are moral entitlements....As such, they should also be legal entitlements or social rights, recognized and protected by law....Rights can be overridden only for compelling moral reasons, like conflicts with other rights, and even then only to the extent necessary."[16] From this statement of the nature of rights, Nash goes on to discuss rights in nature. He notes that "[p]resumably, biotic rights would have something of the same character as human rights, with appropriate modifications to reflect different relational settings."[17] He declares: "I affirm the rights of nonhuman creatures,"[18] while noting some problems others might have with his position. He explains in some detail the reasons for his affirmation:

The stress on nonhuman rights is a way of saying that all life is sacred or intrinsically valuable and worthy of being treated as the subject of human moral consideration. Indeed, the acknowledgment of intrinsic value in nonhuman creatures seems to be implicitly an acknowledgment of their legitimate claims for appropriate treatment from the human community and, therefore, of some level of rights and responsibilities. The underlying concern seems to be human responsibility for nature, and the stress on rights provides an objective moral basis for this responsibility....Advocacy for the rights of nature is the contention that environmental concern is not only an expression of benevolence, but also an obligation of justice—not simply justice to human interests, but also justice to the interests of other creatures. In Western cultures, rights are important; no rights suggest no moral consideration.[19]

Legal rights, then, by formalizing moral rights and concretizing intrinsic value, give some measure of protection to nonhuman nature that would not otherwise occur. Nash goes on to declare that both species and individuals should be respected in a Christian ecological ethic.

While he supports biotic rights, however, in his discussion of the "qualifications of ecological love"[20] Nash opposes the idea of biological egalitarianism as a "moral absurdity" and an "antihuman ideology."[21] He notes the "unique capacities of humans to experience and create moral, spiritual, intellectual, and aesthetic goods," and sees humans' value-creating and value-experiencing capacities as "morally relevant differences" between humans and all other species. As will be explored later, however, human capacities and capabilities can be regarded as complementary goods and contributions to creation, and express complementary—even if, at times in context, competing—intrinsic values. In this understanding, biological egalitarianism is both possible and necessary, to safeguard the life and well-being of all biota.

Nash states further that while other creatures have intrinsic value, "their value is not equal to that of humans. If moral preference for human needs and rights is 'speciesism,' I plead guilty, but I think with just cause."[22] As shall be discussed below, a moral preference for one's own or one's own species' needs and rights need not be "speciesism," but a limited and legitimate self- and species-regard. Nash later relates biotic egalitarianism, moral agency, and graded intrinsic value. He argues again against biotic egalitarianism, and notes that "all creatures are entitled to 'moral consideration,' but not all have the same 'moral significance.' All have intrinsic value, but not equal intrinsic value." He observes that "[t]his ranking mechanism is often considered 'speciesistic' since it gives top moral preference to humans and ranks others descendingly on the basis of the same criteria."[23] Nash goes on to cite approvingly a statement by Herman Daly and John Cobb that "This judgment of intrinsic value is quite different from the judgment of the importance of a species to the interrelated whole."[24]

James Nash, then, strongly endorses nonhuman rights in nature. He qualifies this, to some extent, when he expresses concern for the well-being of the human species and its individual members. He is concerned that human intrinsic value and well-being be carefully considered and advanced in discussions about humans' life as part of nature on Earth, humans' natural rights, and humans' use of Earth's natural goods to meet their needs.

4. Natural Rights in Nature

Nash's "ranking mechanism" for human designation of the extent of intrinsic value inherent in other creatures need not be regarded as "speciesistic," since all species (even without advanced intellectual capabilities or moral agency) favor their own kind, and might be either neutral toward otherkind, or competitors with or predators upon them, and act accordingly. An interesting question here would be whether or not a nonhuman species which in a particular ecosystem did more good for, or less harm to, creation would or should displace the human species at the top of the moral significance grading scale in this context, particularly if in that context the other species had more of the characteristics of the "altruistic predator" and the humans had more of the characteristics of the "profligate predator."

Nash observes rightly that "love entails giving up at least some of our own interests and benefits for the sake of the well-being of others in communal relationships. This mandate applies in both human and ecological communities."[25] He goes on to state that forgiveness, a "fundamental fact of love," is pertinent "only in interactions between moral agents." However, one might argue with this perception utilizing one of Nash's own understandings, namely, that "moral agency" is not to be used to deny rights to other creatures; rather, "moral agents have responsibilities to protect rights. Nonhuman creatures, therefore, can be rights-bearers without being rights-purveyors."[26] Thus, it would seem that ecological love could include forgiveness of nonhuman creatures who have no moral agency. A human fisher, for example, could forgive a hungry bear who chases her away from the salmon she has so arduously brought to shore. A human hiker could forgive a sow bear with cubs who chases him up a tree and consumes the rations he brought along for his wilderness trek. Animals' hunger or defense of their territory in the face of perceived danger to themselves or their offspring are forgivable acts, even when they cause harm. On several occasions, U.S. Forest Service employees have relocated bears or wolves from locales where their predation of human food sources or livestock caused financial hardship; on other occasions, hikers who had been attacked and severely wounded by bears have implored the Forest Service not to kill the bear involved because the latter was acting instinctively to protect themselves, their progeny, or their space.

Similarly, in intraspecies situations, a parent or other adult would forgive a child who unknowingly damages property or inadvertently hurts a sibling. Forgiveness as an expression of love need not require that the one forgiven be morally culpable of the wrongdoing experienced by the one forgiving. The "forgiveness" has to do with neither punishing, nor seeking redress for, another creature's taking of what a human person would see as their own rightful possession: food, freedom to travel responsibly, even life. "Forgiveness" in this sense does not imply that the other has done something objectively wrong, but rather has done something ordinarily wrong in human society. The human as moral agent is saying here that she will not use human understandings (of property rights, for example), human laws, or human power (exercised by an individual with a gun, or by the state on behalf of the individual) to judge and punish (or have punished) nonhumans who are acting appropriately according to their species nature and the natural world context in which the event(s) occurred. Animals' hunger or defense of their territory or offspring, done instinctively and without moral agency as they try to maintain their intrinsic value (however unconsciously), are forgivable acts, even when they cause harm to humans or their property.

Nash need not have supported Daly's and Cobb's separation of judgments on species' intrinsic value and their contextual importance in nature, cited earlier. The theological and sociological affirmation of the human species, in the context from which these writers emerge, does not support such an arbitrary separation of biological reality and ecojustice. On the contrary, it can be "natural," and not species self-hatred, for humans to acknowledge greater contributions and benefits from other species—for example, trees cleanse the air, and provide oxygen for all life—just as it is not unpatriotic to acknowledge that a nation other than one's own is more just and does more for the human community and for human cultural history. This is not meant to be a justification of the misanthropy of some members of groups such as EarthFirst! who question whether humans contribute anything to the Earth, and assert that nothing would be lost if humans were to disappear. Rather, it means that humans should strive harder to fulfill their natural niche in evolving creation, and their role as creation's integrating and caregiving consciousness, while responsibly living up to their capacities in ways Nash described earlier.

Natural rights, then, might be extended beyond human rights in nature to include the rights of all the biotic community—rights recognized, acknowledged, and accepted by humanity. While Nash accepts intrinsic value and rights for all creatures, he qualifies this in context. In his "Bill of Biotic Rights," he declares that "in articulating the rights of 'wild' otherkind, I am in effect defining human responsibilities, since only humans are moral agents capable of respecting rights."[27] Then, when discussing the biotic right "to participate in the natural competition for existence," he expresses a concern with respect to otherkind's right to life:

[T]rophic relationships—members of all species feeding on members of other species—do not allow for a formal right to life of nonhuman individuals. That claim could lead to moral absurdities, such as preventing "bad" predators from feeding on their prey.[28]

While Nash is correct in stating that a "moral absurdity" would occur if all creatures always and absolutely had a "right to life," the absurdity would be eliminated if every creature were acknowledged to have always a formal right to life because of its intrinsic value: in creation as a whole, and in the specific ecosystem of which it is a part. That right to life, in specific contexts and moments, might be denied to an individual creature if another creature views it as a threat to their own existence, or if it has some instrumental value for the survival or well-being of another creature or species. Balancing these values and rights is part of the competition and collaboration, and predator-prey encounters, endemic in an evolutionary world.

An alternative to Nash's concern that he might be guilty of "speciesism" is that one might accept that while all creatures have equal intrinsic value, humans' "moral" preference for human needs and rights would be, in context, a "biological" preference or even a "psychological" or "social" preference. In reality, the preference could be any or all of these, depending on the context. Nash, then, is not guilty of "speciesism," since speciesism is not a "moral preference" but an immoral preference—which Nash does not have—since it suggests dominance over another, not concern and respect for the other—which Nash rightfully advocates. Racism means the attitude and practice of racial domination, sexism means gender domination, and speciesism means species domination; these are all immoral preferences.

As noted earlier, too, Nash states that only humans have moral agency, and that "biotic egalitarianism" is not feasible. One might agree with Nash's evaluation of humans' capacities *vis-a-vis* other creatures, but it would not necessarily follow that other creatures would not be in egalitarian relationships with humans. They, too, have unique capacities, complementary to those of humans, though not, of course, on the same intellectual or moral plane.

Nash notes further that humans, as other creatures, are predators, but since humans alone have moral agency they have the ability to be "altruistic predators" rather than "profligate predators." One might suggest, then, that if humans (individually or as particular communities or as a species), do not live up to the capacities of which they are capable, and are profligate predators, then other species might rightfully react against them because of perceptions of the harm they are doing or might do to other creatures or to the ecosystem. If the ideally "altruistic predators" are in reality "profligate predators," in their particular life-threatened situation they should be treated in an egalitarian manner by otherkind, such that nonhuman species' rights to defend themselves against threats to their survival would be recognized.

The complementary words of Phillip Deere are once again insightful and instructive:

We have to turn around and respect Mother Earth. We cannot say that 'I am just a pilgrim passing through,' so I have no use for the Missouri River. We cannot say that 'I am a Baptist,' 'I am a Methodist,' or 'I am a Catholic,' so I have no use for this tree. We have to understand who we are, what we are, where did we come from. We are the caretakers of this land and we are part of this creation. So we must respect Mother Earth.

When we learned about Christianity we heard about the Father. We learned to pray to the Father, and in the churches every Sunday we heard about Father. To this day we still hear about Father. But we never hear anything about Mother…. But every Indian knows what you mean when you say, "Mother Earth." Traditional people know what you're talking about….We must all learn to say "Mother" as well as we say "our Father." In this way of life we will have balance.

The insights of James Nash prod people to consider carefully their creation context; coexist respectfully with all creatures; and answer their call to creation care—all in the presence of the immanent, creating, and Creator Spirit. Indeed, in such a way of thinking and acting on a sacred Earth in the presence of sacred Being, all humans, all biota, and all creation will be in balance.

ENDNOTES:
[1] James A. Nash, *Loving Nature: Ecological Integrity and Christian Responsibility* (Nashville, TN: Abingdon, 1991), 140.
[2] Nash, 152-59.
[3] Nash, 171.
[4] Nash, 186-89.
[5] Nash, 110.
[6] This and subsequent quotes from Phillip Deere are taken from the author's interviews with him in Great Falls, Montana, October, 1984; and in his home in Okemah, Oklahoma, June, 1985, where I stayed with him shortly before he died. An in-depth elaboration of his life

and work and how it complements that of Francis of Assisi is found in John Hart, *Sacramental Commons: Christian Ecological Ethics* (Lanham, MD: Rowman and Littlefield, 2006), chapter 4: "Native Spirits," 45-57.

[7] The analysis that follows is adapted, in part, from my presentation "Salmon and Social Ethics" at the Society of Christian Ethics Annual Meeting, Vancouver, B.C., Canada, January 2002. Subsequently, it was published as "Salmon and Social Ethics: Relational Consciousness in the Web of Life," *Journal of the Society of Christian Ethics*, Vol. 22 (Fall, 2002): 67-93. Ideas were developed further in Hart (2006), *Sacramental Commons: Christian Ecological Ethics*, for which Nash wrote a cover endorsement. From the Vancouver meeting, I retain one of my favorite memories of my friendship with Jim. We walked through the streets engaged in conversation, and had dinner together.

[8] Nash, 139.
[9] Nash, 140.
[10] Nash, 140-41.
[11] Nash, 143.
[12] Nash, 141
[13] Nash, 111.
[14] Nash, 112.
[15] Nash, 137.
[16] Nash, 169.
[17] Nash, 170.
[18] Nash, 173.
[19] Nash, 175.
[20] Nash, 149-51.
[21] Nash, 149.
[22] Nash, 150.
[23] Nash, 181.
[24] Nash, 182.
[25] Nash, 150.
[26] Nash, 170.
[27] Nash, 186.
[28] Nash, 186-7.

James A. Nash: Mentoring for Action/Reflection

By Marla Marcum

After several years and scores of respectable excuses about why I wasn't the right person for the job, I finally got involved with the grassroots climate movement. In May 2009, I began a leave of absence from studies in Social and Ecological Ethics at Boston University School of Theology. I took this leave in order to work as a full-time volunteer organizer, building bridges between the youth climate movement, local climate action groups, and communities of faith–three groups whose core values are remarkably resonant and whose resources are dramatically different–and thus, complementary. I expect to return to my studies in the Fall of 2011, when I'll start thinking more systematically about what I've learned in the field.

This essay combines my remarks from an event held in honor of Jim Nash on the eve of the fortieth Earth Day with some additional reflections on the importance of his work for the emerging grassroots climate movement. Unlike many of the other tributes, mine was conversational in tone and rough around the edges, and I maintain that tone and those edges in this essay.

I learned from Jim Nash that sometimes the truths that are most worth telling are the ones that nobody wants to hear. That privilege and comfort are poor excuses for inaction. That I need to be willing to risk my own significance and position so that I can speak and act in ways that promote the common good. These lessons inspired me to challenge the assumptions of one of the speakers and then to offer the following thoughts that night:

April 21, 2010
It is difficult for me to be here tonight, and I'm still not sure I made the right choice. I should be somewhere else and so should all of you. If Jim Nash were with us today, I know where he would be.

You see, tonight on the Boston Common, hundreds of people are gathered to protest the fact that we live within a system that forces us to participate in the destruction of our own futures. Unless we are very wealthy, we have little choice about how the energy we use is generated and distributed. The lamp on any bedside table is powered by dirty electricity. The same lamp that enables a parent to read a bedtime story to a child in hopes that she will stay curious, become a good student, grow up to get a job that pays a living wage—that same lamp is powered almost completely by the burning of fossil fuels at a time when we know that we have passed the safe upper limit of carbon in our atmosphere. And so, the climate is already changing.

In lectures, Jim Nash often claimed that in the future, all ethics will be ecological ethics. When the biophysical systems upon which we depend for our survival are threatened, then every realm of our being also is threatened. A stable climate is the foundation of a stable society. We now live in a time when our most mundane actions result in emissions that further destabilize the climate. We did not intend this outcome, but we are going to have to find a way to face it and to change. If we do not act quickly, the conditions that make even partial justice and peace possible will be undermined.

The group now gathered on the Boston Common calls itself The Leadership Campaign, and we are calling for 100% clean electricity in Massachusetts by 2020. Last fall, this student-led movement looked for inspiration to an earlier movement also led by young people. When people saw black students sitting peacefully at a segregated lunch counter in Greensboro, NC in 1960, the message was clear. At the most basic level, that message was: *we have the right to be here. You (lunch counter operators) have the power to serve us lunch.*

Likewise, we chose to Sleep Out. Although we are ratepayers, we cannot control how our homes, dorms, or apartments are powered. We chose to Sleep Out on the Boston Common[1] because the state legislature has the power to determine how electricity is generated and distributed. The Sleep Outs were a successful tactic for our campaign last fall.[2]

Tomorrow is the 40th Earth Day. If we do not act to reduce our CO2 emissions swiftly and dramatically, those gathered on the 100th earth Day will curse us, but they might not be able to do it in Boston because much of Boston may be under water.

We chose Earth Day (to wake up on the Boston Common or in holding cells)[3] because it's an iconic day—the 40th Earth Day—and we believe that although clean-ups and other community-based actions are important on Earth Day, the ecological realities we face call for a proportionate response. We need to step up our game to ensure a just and stable future for all.

I spend a lot of time asking myself what Jim Nash would do or say in a particular situation. I think he *would* be present at a tribute event tonight if we were honoring one of his mentors–Muelder or Deats–but I'm also convinced that he would be down on the Boston Common with his tent, bolstering the hopes of the (mostly young) people who have turned out to call for 100% clean electricity in ten years.

I remember Nash refusing to take on a full teaching load at the School of Theology because he was a "working ethicist." He needed the freedom and the time to do that work. His commitment to that professional decision made an impression on me. Nash would be on the Boston Common tonight, encouraging those gathered to trust their convictions and to call for the solutions we need, even if that means finding the courage to demand something that seems completely absurd in the given political and economic climate. We need solutions proportionate to the biophysical realities that we have created through our own ways of being in the world. I learned from Jim Nash that we have to incorporate all relevant facts into our ethical thought, teaching, and action. The "politically possible" can no longer be the cornerstone of our common life–the fact upon which we construct our lives together in the future.

In light of all this, Nash would remind everyone on the Common that we'd better be ready to work for the futures we envision, noting that "right makes might" about as often as "might makes right". If it is not possible to change the way we power our lives, then we'd better get to work to change the conditions that determine what's possible.

Jim Antal and I attended the first part of the rally on the Common tonight before joining you here, and I'll be headed back there when we're finished. I have extra tent space and extra sleeping gear if any of you want to join me. At age 35, I spent 31 nights from October 24th to December 7th sleeping outside. Boston University School of Theology's Dean Mary Elizabeth Moore slept out with us on a brick plaza at Boston University in freezing weather. Rev. Dr. Jim Antal and a few other clergy slept out with us on the Common in their clerical collars, knowing they were risking arrest. Of course, this is not the only way to join the grassroots movement for climate solutions, but I am certain that Jim Nash would have been there with his tent.

And I can promise you that when people over the age of fifty show up to work for a better future, the younger people notice. Most of them can expect to be alive in 80 years, and they are not used to seeing people your age commit to working *with* them to safeguard their futures.

What resources do *you* have that young people lack? If you're a church leader, one simple answer is your church building. Congregations all over Massachusetts have opened their doors to our work, allowing us to sleep on the floor, prepare meals, and meet in their churches in exchange for the kind of work around the building that a large group of young people can do. In January, forty college students held a week-long retreat in the United Methodist Church in Winthrop. Some of them had never been in a church before the Sleep Outs began.

Because of this work, and regardless of their faith traditions, hundreds of college students in secular Massachusetts know from experience that when they are working for justice, the churches are their natural partners. They have experience communicating with people of faith about their shared values, and they know their way around the church kitchen. Having figured out what kinds of questions to ask about how a congregation is organized and what members believe, some will drop in on adult Sunday School to hear what the classes are talking about, and I've walked into more than one church to see a handful of climate activists – who range from atheist to estranged from the church of their youth – singing with the choir. This shift in attitude toward the churches has been swift and stunning, and it only took a little creative thinking and the willingness to offer hospitality and non-monetary support to some values-driven young people.

Jim Nash showed me that my deepest impulses about faithful living and loving *belonged* in the classroom and in our ethical analysis of the world around us. When a thing is absurd, let's call it absurd. It is absurd that we are gathered here tonight to honor a man who loved the whole creation so much while the whole thing is burning and sinking beneath the waves. I learned from Jim that it would be completely foolish to let this opportunity pass–all of us gathered together at one moment. Whatever your commitments to work for justice, if we don't solve our climate problem, all of our other efforts will be rendered meaningless. We should not be here. We should be on the Boston Common.

I have come to believe that Nash's approach to ethical method both *describes* the best moral decision-making at work within vibrant grassroots movements and *offers* tools for moral imagination that could allow coalitions of diverse constituencies to live into a more the future together. I'll have a lot of work to do, but Nash's creative hybrid of the rigorous synoptic-analytic method of the Boston Personalists with some strains of virtue ethics enables the creation of a system of guiding virtues that can be shared and applied consistently by coalition partners with widely differing theological commitments, while making space for each constituency to develop theological interpretations of the virtues for in-group use only. Grassroots organizing work is all about relationships. Organizers build coalitions and create bonds of trust and mutual commitment across many lines of historic division and mistrust. Nash's method offers a way to craft a shared vision for the way things ought to be–one that is authentic to everyone in the coalition. Such a shared vision can be a source of realistic hope in our ability to transform the impossible into the possible.

Nash's method is not an easy or quick way to impart moral wisdom, but it may be the among best ways to nurture virtuous citizens of the world in an uncertain time. As we search for solutions, we need to remember that there will be no truly easy answers. If someone offers you a silver bullet, it's probably just a bullet.

I'm here tonight because I could not bear to forego the opportunity to honor Jim in the presence of his family, his colleagues, and my fellow students. Of course, I am not suggesting that I am the only one here tonight that seeks to honor Jim's memory and to live out a life of integrity through action.

I came to Boston University School of Theology ten years ago feeling certain that I wanted to be an ethicist, but I was fully aware that I also had no idea what that meant. I was guessing that – whatever the way of the ethicist was – it might be the way that I could continue to learn and grow and work for justice in the world. I had never heard of Jim Nash when I applied, but I was overjoyed to see "Christian Ecology and Politics" on the list of course offerings for my second semester.

When I read Nash's "ecological autobiography"[4] on the first day of class, I realized that my professor came from a background similar to mine. I'm sure he wasn't the only member of the faculty who came from a working class family, but he was certainly the only one I had yet encountered who was proud of it. He demonstrated the same kind of connection to the land and understanding of peoples' struggles that I felt. He knew them and he loved them. Jim showed me that courage is not folly, especially when it compels us to act in love.

Without Jim Nash, I'm not sure I'd know what it means (or can mean) to be an ethicist. I couldn't figure out how to *be* in this place. The roles laid out before me didn't make sense and I couldn't make myself fit in. As the second person from any part of the family to go to college and the first to even think about graduate school, I didn't have many models for how I might hold on to those roots as I pushed myself in the academy. I had found a model.

Nash showed me how I could be a feminist with a principled moral and theological stand on a woman's right to choose. When he told stories of his work with the Massachusetts Council of Churches, I saw that he was the same unflinching and unapologetic champion for what he knew was right in that professional setting. But he was also thoughtful, a deep listener, and one who refused to take himself too seriously. His laughter could fill a room no less than his impassioned call for right action. He changed his mind (and admitted it) when he got new information that was persuasive. He wanted to know what we thought, but he never let our assumptions go unchallenged. He worked from his gut, and his capacity for love was enormous. He loved the world – even the ugly parts. He loved it all so much that he spent a lot of time being angry about the way things were. That loving anger drove him, and he recognized right away that mine drove me too. He told me to cultivate that rage, and he urged me to use it in my work, assuring me that as long as my rage flowed from a place of love, it would serve the world much better than any attempts I might make at pretending to have a placid heart so that others would not be upset by my anger.

What a relief! I do *not* have a placid heart. Jim Nash's understanding words gave me permission to engage the world from places that drive me to act. He affirmed my suspicion that love is nothing if not a verb. I could never thank him enough for these gifts.

ENDNOTES

[1] The Boston Common sits directly in front of the Massachusetts State Capitol building.

[2] We chose electricity because it will be easier to reduce carbon emissions in the transportation and heating sectors in Massachusetts if we have access to clean electricity. For additional information on the platform, partner organizations, and progress of The Leadership Campaign, www.theleadershipcampaign.org and Students for a Just and Stable Future www.justandstable.org, www.newenglandclimatesummer.org, http://climatesummer.wordpress.com/. In Fall 2009, our campaign focused on the Sleep Out tactic. We slept out for 42 nights from October 24th to December 7th. On Sunday nights people from across the state (mostly students) slept out on the Boston Common. On Monday mornings, we packed up our gear, stashed it in the Church on the Hill (where we had 24 hour access to restroom facilities, coffee, and fellowship with church members), and then we headed into the State House to visit legislators and advocate for our cause. On December 7th, the first day of the climate talks in Copenhagen, leaders from the Global Warming and Climate Change committees of the house and senate introduced our bill.

[3] We had hoped that the 40th Earth Day would dawn with Massachusetts well on its way to a clean electricity future. Instead, our Sleep Out on April 21, 2010 was one of many pressure tactics planned for April 21-22 to force our bill out of the House Ethics and Rules Committee, where it had languished since January because of an unrelated political dispute between the legislator who filed the bill that we wrote and the Chair of that committee. The Sleep Outs had

been used in the Fall to generate awareness and grow the campaign, to educate the public and legislators, to attract media coverage, and to apply pressure to specific leaders to take actions in support of the Campaign. This time, we expected to be arrested for misdemeanor trespassing at the Sleep Out, and the legislator we were targeting knew that if arrested, we'd be explaining to the media that he was holding up a bill that could re-power Massachusetts with clean energy and green jobs on the 40th Earth Day. It is illegal to be on the Boston Common after 11pm. More than 220 individuals have already been through the courts on charges of trespassing for our Sleep Outs in Fall 2009 (most on multiple citations). Those charged with misdemeanor trespassing in the Fall had been fined and told that "there would be handcuffs" next time. The night of the Jim Nash tribute was "next time".

[4] The ecological autobiography appears in the Introduction to Nash's *Loving Nature: Ecological Integrity and Christian Responsibility* (Nashville, TN: Abingdon Press, 1991)

Biotic Rights and Political Ecology:
James A. Nash's Ecological Vision and Lessons from Zimbabwe

By Shandirai Mawokomatanda

Introduction

In his book *Loving Nature*,[1] James Nash offers us a vision for "ecological integrity and Christian responsibility" toward nature. Speaking out of his Wesleyan tradition, Nash presents how "love is the integrating center of the whole Christian faith and ethics"[2] and how a Christian ecological ethics is deficient and inconceivable if it is not grounded in Christian love. He defines his conception of love in a multi-dimensional manner, which includes love as beneficence, other-esteem, receptivity, humility, understanding, communion, and justice.[3] Nash then argues that love intimately relates to concerns for justice, and how justice concerns matters of rights and responsibilities.[4]

Nash's connection of love with justice, primarily his understanding of love as ecological justice, has political implications. My presentation explores the political dimensions of Nash's ecological vision. Although Nash explores the implications of his ecological vision on political economy, he focuses less on political ecology. Political ecology concerns itself with the complex relations between nature and society; that is, human political activity in society can be contingent on changes in the environment in the same way that changes in the environment are contingent on human political activity. My presentation will offer the case study in Zimbabwe as an example of how changes in the environment can lead to a political movement which is able to transform the political activity of a society.

People, Politics and Public Policy in Ecology

In *Loving Nature*, James Nash offers 8 biotic rights as part of Bill of Biotic rights. For Nash, these rights articulate the just claims that inhere in nonhuman species and their members. As a result, human beings have a moral responsibility to safeguard these biotic rights. In order to discern how biotic rights connect with ecological concerns in Africa, my presentation addresses only one of the eight rights presented by Nash. The eighth right in Nash's Bill of Biotic Rights states that members of the biotic community have "*the right to redress through human interventions, to restore a semblance of the natural conditions disrupted by human actions.*"[5] I applaud this statement for expressing pragmatic political concerns. James Nash was a politically astute individual. He was a pragmatist and a politician, in the best sense of the word. He understood that ethics, including environmental ethics, had political implications. For this reason, he concludes *Loving Nature* by offering some political directions for ecological integrity. Politics, according to Nash, is "an essential means for realizing the desirable."

Politics is not only about the mastery of the methods of power... politics is about the responsible use of power to bring ethical goals like justice to fruition. Ethically, politics is the way that a pluralistic society ought to govern itself in order to insure that all parties in conflict have a say in decisions, to conciliate rival interests, and to advance social peace and justice. It is a means not only of controlling social evils, but also of promoting the general welfare.[6]

Nash goes on to argue how the essential moral problem is not the presence of politics in society, but rather the absence or perversion of politics. While Nash argues against anthropocentrism throughout *Loving Nature*, he still ultimately resorts to anthropogenic means of redressing ecological crises.

Nash is realistic in observing the anthropogenic means of redressing ecological problems. That is, Nash is rational to observe that human beings have a responsibility to redress and resolve problems caused by humans with the environment. Public policy is the political domain he concludes as having the most effective means for resolving ecological problems. The political directions he concludes with relate primarily to the standards by which ecologically sound and morally responsible public policy ought to have. No doubt that Nash's focus on public policy is an expression of his commitment to the work of the Center for Public Policy with which he worked. However, the conclusion that the human community is ultimately responsible – through "human interventions" – to redress ecological problems, as the eighth biotic right states, neglects an important role that the environment itself plays as a political party.

While Nash's whole argument rests on asserting the intrinsic value of nature from which his biotic rights stem, one question to ask is regarding nature's role in politics. If one is to assert the presence of biotic rights, how does nature or the environment act in the political discourse? And how does one account for the role that nature or the environment plays in politics? The answers to these questions may be found in the developing discourse in the field of political ecology.

People, Politics and Political Ecology:
The field of political ecology is one that has been concerned with the complex relations between nature and society. In political ecology, not only can changes in the environment be contingent on human political activity, but human political activity in society can also be contingent on changes in the environment. Originally, scholars in the field sought to analyze the forms of access and control over resources (human and natural) and implications for ecological integrity. Traditionally, political ecology seeks "to expose flaws in dominant approaches to the environment favored by corporate, state, and international authorities, working to demonstrate the undesirable impacts of policies and market conditions, especially from the point of view of local people, marginal groups, and vulnerable populations."[7] Political ecology thus enters the "power politics" discourse by asserting that changes to the environment are often contingent outcomes of power imbalances, primarily in the human community. As such, the original thrust in political ecology saw changes in the environment as being contingent on human political activity; however, an integrative political ecology now sees the natural environment as a political unit itself.

Political ecology concerns itself with the interdependence and interrelationships between human political units and their natural environment. There are four main theses of political ecology that try to explain the complex nature of relations between nature/ the environment and society.[8] One thesis tries to explain environmental "change" using a narrative of degradation and marginalization. For example, land degradation, long blamed on marginal people, is put in a larger political and economic context.[9] Political economy, which Nash deals with in *Loving Nature*, becomes central to discerning ecological integrity and human responsibility.

A second thesis, although related to the first, tries to explain problems in environmental "access" using a narrative of environmental conflict. That is, "Environmental conflicts are shown to be part of larger gendered, classed, and raced struggles and vice versa."[10] Existing and long-term conflict within and between human communities are given ecological dimensions through human environmental policies and practices. This second thesis relates to a third, which tries to explain the dynamics of social upheaval in ecological terms. Using a narrative of environmental identity and social movement, "political and social struggles are shown to be linked to basic issues of livelihood and environmental protection."[11] Here, changes in environmental control, management, or conditions are seen as creating opportunities, and sometimes imperatives, for local groups to secure and represent themselves politically.

A fourth thesis examines the dynamics of failures in conservation and control processes. This fourth thesis connects, for me, to Nash's eighth biotic right. As human efforts to redress ecological problems fail, the fourth thesis hints at the political dimensions of an environment that acts back on human communities and, at the least, does not always bend to the will of human activity without protest. The most convincing example of this phenomenon is the effects of global warming and global climate change. Scientists studying changes in the global climate accredit it to the impact of human activity. Now, political movements in response to global climate change are beginning to find momentum arguing that, if the human community does not change its behavior, the results will be catastrophic. The argument can thus be made that nature is beginning to act back and some, in society, have taken the political mandate and lead from nature itself to act on behalf of and with nature.

Whereas the first three theses are largely concerned with relations between the environment and human political units, the fourth thesis in political ecology helps to assert the possibility of viewing nature or the environment as a political unit itself. That is, examining the dynamics of environmental change to include nature's impact on human activity leads to the proposal of a fifth thesis. A fifth thesis would explore the dynamics of how nature can be viewed as a political unit with the political capacity to act back on society. Such a thesis would resonate with Nash's argument for the necessity of biotic rights. The use of rights language belongs in the domain of politics; politics being the means to promote the general welfare, which includes the welfare of the natural environment.

Nash's presentation of biotic rights is ingenious because he opens the door for political ecologist to examine how nature or the environment acts in the political discourse. He points to the important of a fifth thesis, in political ecology, that seeks to account for the role that nature or the environment plays in politics. Inevitably, this fifth thesis will be related to the third thesis which finds environmental changes creating imperatives for local groups to represent themselves politically. The argument can be made that human beings can stand in solidarity and in community with the natural environment as they try to redress environmental problems, promoting human and ecological wellbeing together.

In the following discussion I will engage the discourse in political ecology to examine the nature of the interdependence and interrelationships between human political units and their natural environment. In particular, I will engage the roles of religious communities in Zimbabwe as political units, acting in response to and on behalf of the natural environment; but, more importantly, recognizing the environment as having rights which need to be safeguarded. I will posit this as having the potential of transforming the landscape of political ecology in Africa.

Lessons from Zimbabwe in Political Ecology:
The following discussion explores the struggles over knowledge, power and practice as consequently relating to ecological conflict. Ecological conflict describes not only ecological dimension of human conflict but also the conflict between the humanity and the natural environment. That is, not only do political processes have consequences on the environment, but changes in the environment have political consequences as well. A case study in Zimbabwe can help illustrate the dynamics of this conflict, and the subsequent role of human political units in transforming the conflict. I wish to do so in order to point out how the religious environmental movements of tree planting in Zimbabwe cannot make a lasting impact without incorporating the political dimensions of ecological integrity.

In the mid-1990s, Zimbabwe began a controversial Land Reform program that sought to transfer white-owned farmlands to native black Zimbabweans. The program was largely politically motivated but having wider consequences, including ecological, socio-economic and political.[12] While the land reform program, allegedly, sought to address the plight of the poor in Zimbabwe, the actual political process did quite the opposite.[13] Poor communities living in rural areas largely felt the environmental effects of the political process. The political situation in Zimbabwe led to a declining economy with the highest inflation rates in the world being recorded in the country. The crashing economy destabilized many social, economic, and political institutions leading to an increase in unemployment rates where three-fourths of the nation was unemployed. The high rates in unemployment led some to assume methods of subsistence living, which meant returning to a way of life increasingly dependent on the natural environment for an already marginal population. Whereas electricity has supplied the power for cooking stoves in the cities, for instance, the harvesting of firewood became a necessary alternative no longer for rural communities alone but also urban inhabitants. Whereas the raising of livestock had once sustained a meat diet for many people, the turned economy led some to resort to wildlife hunting, a practice that had been left to the marginal poor of the country.

With nearly half of Zimbabwe's poor living in marginal rural areas, the environment had already been in crisis long before the land reform program. The land reform program in Zimbabwe only exacerbated a political process that had begun with post independence development policies supported by the World Bank and IMF. As a result, some religious communities in Zimbabwe began to respond to the nation's environmental crisis. Since rural communities felt the stress of environmental changes, leaders of Zimbabwean traditional religion and independent churches began offering a response employing their religious-spiritual resources to motivate people for ecological action.[14] They appealed to traditional, cultural, and theological teachings for environmental integrity.[15] Marthinus Daneel describes one such movement in Zimbabwe.

In Zimbabwe, religious leaders sought to exercise their spiritual authority over modern processes of land and community development because they understood themselves to be custodians of the land. Once they had been central and instrumental to the struggle of political liberation and independence; however, after independence, they found themselves relatively isolated and marginalized by the very political government they had supported. "They felt powerless to do much about the problems of their people – continuing landlessness, poverty, increasing population pressure on already overcrowded communal lands, deterioration of the environment resulting in scarcities of fuel wood and poor crop yields, and so on."[16] Out of this experience, they were moved to organize and mobilize their constituents to address the political and environmental issues they faced.

Appealing to the rhetoric that had gained them eminence during the liberation struggle, traditional religion and independent church religious communities "declared war" on deforestation and on ecological destruction.[17] Whereas the quest to reclaim lost land had been a part of the slogan for the political liberation struggle, the healing of the wounded land became the new slogan in the ecological liberation war. To this end, various institutions, such as the Association of Zimbabwean Traditional Ecologists and the Zimbabwean Institute for Religious Research and Ecological Conservation, were established to guide the process. While these institutions collaborated with other governmental and non-governmental institutions, when possible, they remained independent and operated independently.

It is unclear what role these religious communities and institutions played during the land reform program of the mid-nineties. It is unclear to how they responded to the revival of the slogan to reclaim lost lands, which was part of the political land reform program. Certainly they must have had a stake in the process especially when the same rural communities were impacted the most by the social, economic and ecological downturn that followed. Perhaps, it is here that Nash's vision for public policy may be useful for the Zimbabwean context. Nash concludes that public policy is the one political domain best equipped to engage ecological issues and, thus, offers guidelines with which to construct "ecologically sound and morally responsible public policy." Zimbabwe would have benefited from a land reform policy informed by the principles Nash outlines. The discourse in political ecology is also helpful to the Zimbabwean case. Studies in political ecology inform how religious communities in Zimbabwe could have been a powerful political unit to counter a land reform policy that was not ecologically sound or morally responsible. Religious communities could have capitalized on their moral, social, and political capital to engage the governmental parties in constructing a meaningful land reform policy. It is arguable to what extent the government had the wellbeing of the poor in mind when they issued the land reform policy; however, had religious communities understood themselves as political units with a stake in the nation's public policy – something which they must have understood but had not capitalized on – they might have sought ways to actively and pro-actively engage the formation of ecologically sound and morally responsible public policy.

In addition, the fifth thesis in political ecology, which identifies nature as a political unit itself, might be a useful and motivating principle from which religious communities, especially traditional religions, can operate. Although traditional religious leadership understand themselves as custodians of the land, who may act on behalf of the land, it is also important to recognize how the land acts back itself, and protests the destructive activity of humans on the environment. How the land's custodian act must be in concert with the political movement of the natural environment. In an African religious worldview, it is certainly conceivable to have a theology that understands God, the ancestors, or the Spirit/spirits as giving agency to the land to act back in protest to a sinning or failing humanity. By appealing to the mandate to heal the wounded and lost lands, leaders in religious communities certainly understood the interdependence of relations between society, the environment, and the divine/spiritual realm.

Conclusion

Although I personally did not study with James Nash, I find him to be a model public figure whose political vision and pragmatic concerns for ecological integrity inspires Christian responsibility. Combined with lessons learned in political ecology where human community and the natural environment share political commitments to human and ecological wellbeing, Nash's political and pragmatic approach to environmental ethics provides for an integral response to the world's most pressing ecological needs. As the world's political leaders gather in a series of summits to discern our global response to global climate change, Nash's vision offers important principles to guide the political deliberations and policies coming out of these summits. However, political ecology reminds us that there are many political actors with a stake in any public policy concerning the environment. Local communities and marginal groups, including religious communities have a stake in the outcome of the policy making process and, more importantly, the environment itself has a stake. Political ecology reminds us that the environment is itself a political actor with a mandate that human political units discern how to account for the role that nature or the environment plays in politics. Political ecology connects the wellbeing of the environment to the wellbeing of a people because discerning the wellbeing of a people is to engage in politics; that is, political ecology engages in a public discourse, practice, and process seeking to promote the common and "commons good."[18] Nash's work in environmental ethics provides an enduring legacy for how Christian communities can responsibly participate in this political and ecological process.

ENDNOTES
[1] James Nash, *Loving Nature: Ecological Integrity and Christian Responsibility* (Nashville, TN: Abingdon Press, 1991).
[2] Nash, 139. The idea that love is the integrating center of all Christian faith resonates with what John Wesley taught. Wesley's doctrine of Christian Perfection had love as the *telos* for Christian discipleship.
[3] Ibid, 139-161.
[4] Ibid, 162-191.
[5] Ibid, 188.
[6] Ibid, 192.
[7] See Paul Robbins, *Political Ecology: A Critical Introduction* (Malden, MA: Blackwell Publishing, 2004), pp. 13.
[8] The four theses described here are explained by Paul Robbins in his introductory text in political ecology. These four these correspond with the historical development in political ecology.
[9] Ibid., 14.
[10] Ibid.
[11] Ibid.
[12] For an analysis of the implication of the land acquisition program in Zimbabwe, see Sam Moyo, "The Political Economy of Land Acquisition and Redistribution in Zimbabwe: 1990-1999," *Journal of Southern African Studies*, Volume 26, No.1 (March 2000), pp.5-28.
[13] Over six million indigenous black people, almost half the population, live in Zimbabwe's marginal rural lands, the communal areas. These areas have poor soils and unreliable rainfall; producers lack control of water rights and are excluded from the bulk of the nations' natural resources.
[14] Studies in African Religion typically show that African Traditional Religions (ATR) and African Independent Churches (AIC) have their largest constituents living in rural communities.

[15] For a description of the religious response of traditional religion and independent church in Zimbabwe, see Marthinus Daneel, *African Earthkeepers: Wholistic Interfaith Mission* (Maryknoll, NY: Orbis Books, 2001).

[16] Ibid., 40

[17] Ibid., 42

[18] John Hart introduces this concept of a Commons Good in his work, *Sacramental Commons: Christian Ecological Ethics* (New York, NY: Rowman & Littlefield, 2006).

James A. Nash, Ecofeminism, and Getting Our Hands Dirty

By Tallessyn Zawn Grenfell-Lee

It was a true honor and privilege to experience James A. Nash as a teacher and mentor. His enthusiasm, passion, and *compassion* were contagious. In the classroom, Jim not only inspired this kind of response from students; but he also had a powerful approach to ethics, incorporating a dedication to sound theology, the insistence on rigorous analysis, and a keen awareness the nuances of current political and social issues. These features of his integrative approach inspired my current work in eco-feminism.

In true Wesleyan fashion, Jim approached ethics as a synthetic, integrative, dialectic balance among poles and priorities. For example, he was fully committed to both science and ethics. He argued:

The field of ethics needs scientific evidence to make decisions. Moral norms are valid based on how they enable humans and other species to thrive. On the other hand, scientists must heed the degree to which they are dependent upon ethical assumptions without even recognizing it. Risk is not a scientific term, but a moral term: you are making judgments about what is harmful or good.[1]

Jim also liked to talk about love and justice. He understood the shallow, unsustainable nature of discussions of love, and expressions of love, in the absence of the dimension of justice. He said, "I don't want to separate love and justice; justice is an expression of love. If you can't be just with me, forget the rest of your benevolence. Everything else is gravy. Justice is the embryonic form of love." Jim was even toying with the idea of defining sin fundamentally as injustice. He argued, "Sin is seeking our own good, as individuals, families, nations, or species, at the expense of the good of others. Depriving them of their *due*." Jim felt that the alienation that occurs, which he called "breaking the bonds with God and our comrades in Creation," is actually the consequence of the sin; the real sin is injustice. Therefore, sin is inherently relational: a broken covenant with self, God, other, and nature.

All these ideas – questioning scientism and elitism, integrating love and justice, justice and sin, sin and relationships, relationships and nature – fit well within the approach of eco-feminism, which seeks to understand ecological destruction and healing relationally, in the context of systems and theologies of hierarchy and exploitation. Jim fully supported the necessary perspectives and critiques eco-feminism offers to the exploration of ecological ethics. At a time when many still considered eco-feminism a distraction and not worth serious consideration,[2] Jim strongly and directly criticized this view as erroneous and disrespectful of other perspectives. When Jim was accused of being mean-spirited, he laughed and responded that all the *women* he had consulted agreed that he could and probably should have been much harsher in his critique.

Controversies aside, Jim was excited to see what directions eco-feminism would travel as it moved forward into the future. Hindu eco-feminist and physicist Vandana Shiva has brought to light the ways the global food industry is destroying the ecosystems and ways of life of people around the globe, and particularly in India, where forces such as trade liberalization and corporate globalization, through the so-called "Green Revolution," have led to widespread farm bankruptcy; 200,000 of these farmers have committed suicide since 1997 as a result.[3] 200,000 members of the family of God have been driven to suicide in India alone. How have we played a part? How do our policies, theologies, and personal choices create or sustain such an exploitative, destructive system? Jim used to say, we're really focused on the "liberty" but we as a society often ignore or forget the "justice" and the "for all."

There are obvious ecological dimensions to this humanitarian crisis: Green Revolution farming practices destroy topsoil, water, sustainable holistic agricultural systems, biodiversity, and various habitats. But when people hear the word "farmers," how many of us picture men in our minds? We assume that men farm; women just garden. Yet in less industrialized areas of the world, where about 70 percent of the people make a living by farming, up to 80 percent of these farmers are women. Yet women are often excluded from farmers associations and unions, as well as from land tenure and access to credit.[4] The effects of climate change, free trade, and global agribusiness destabilizes the livelihoods of these women, forcing a certain percentage of them to seek alternative sources of income, such as prostitution.[5]

Eco-feminism has something important to contribute to ecological ethics. As I began to ask what can we do to address these ethical issues, I remembered how Jim was intrigued by the idea of ecological conversion experiences—what causes them, and how do they impact our lifestyles and churches? I've recently begun to examine our spiritual relationship with the earth in terms of the physical interaction found in farming and gardening. I've started to study the idea of rolling up our sleeves and getting our hands dirty as a path toward kinship, toward ecological conversion. What happens to local communities, theologies, and concepts of justice when a church family integrates farming and gardening into its understanding of discipleship? When churches reach out to their communities and support local, sustainable, organic food as they nurture kinship and healing?

Eco-feminism rejects the dualisms that say ultimate spiritual awakening involves wholly separating from the physical, earthly realm into some supposedly higher, transcendent realm. Rather, ultimate spiritual awakening, healing, kinship, comes from rediscovering our rootedness in the soil of the earth, the dirty, messy Body of God, which connects us to all other life on earth. Ecological conversion means we finally see ourselves as part of an ecosystem, and realize that in order to meet the demands of justice, all our actions—spiritual, political, personal, communal—must reflect this rootedness, this embeddedness. In Garden Earth, we are literally each other's keepers!

Jim also loved to talk about frugality. In contrast to scarcity, Jim's interpretation of this virtue focused on its Latin root, which means fruitfulness and joyfulness. Getting our hands dirty can be seen as a chore; maybe we'd rather wash off and continue to try to deny our finitude—deny that someday, we'll be going back to the Body with a capital B. But if we experience true conversion, frugality *is* fruitfulness—abundant, joyful, fullness of life in community, solidarity, and kinship with the whole earth. Isn't *that* what the kin-dom is all about?

It is a real honor to carry on Jim's legacy today. I'd like to close with the end of Jim's final lecture to his class on Christian Social Ethics. Even though he spoke these words years ago, I still find them inspiring today, especially in the face of such overwhelming challenges as the ecological crisis, and the destruction of the global military-industrial-capitalistic complex, which seems so large, with so much momentum, that it's hard to imagine how we will turn it around. But the words of hope with which he left us are these:

The present prospects are bleak; but we are not fated. Possibilities *can* be transformed. Sin is not the only *or the primary* feature of humanity. There is also a strong, although belittled, potential for *good*, empowered by common grace. Social reform requires an acute consciousness of human sin *and* confidence in human goodness.[6]

ENDNOTES

[1] Nash citations come from Boston University School of Theology lectures: TS829: Christian Ecological Ethics and Political Issues, Spring 2004; TS845: Christian Social Ethics, Spring 2003.

[2] Thomas Sieger Derr, James A. Nash, and Richard John Neuhaus, *Environmental Ethics and Christian Humanism*, Abingdon Press Studies in Christian Ethics and Economic Life (Nashville,: Abingdon Press, 1996), 50ff.

[3] Vandana Shiva, "Why Are Indian Farmers Committing Suicide and How Can We Stop This Tragedy?" *Voltaire. edition internationale*, May 23 2009.

[4] Data from the Worldwatch Institute, worldwatch.org.

[5] According to Suneeta Mukherjee of the United Nations Population Fund: Joseph Holandes Ubalde, "Climate Change Pushes Poor Women to Prostitution, Dangerous Work," *GMANews. TV,* November 19 2009.

[6] Nash citations come from Boston University School of Theology lectures: TS829: Christian Ecological Ethics and Political Issues, Spring 2004; TS845: Christian Social Ethics, Spring 2003.

Canary in a Coal Mine: T
he Critical Task for the Christian Church

By James Antal

I am honored to have the opportunity to add my voice to this chorus of praise for the visionary work of James A. Nash. And I am grateful to others for detailing many of the specific contributions which Nash made as a major early contributor to the emerging field of environmental ethics. I was a beneficiary of the earlier witness advanced by Paul Santmire, Norm Faramelli, Scott Paradise, Holmes Rolston III, and others. Much of my life's work – in the church, the peace and justice movement, and the academy – emerges from their insights and questions.

Although Jim Nash and I met in the mid 1980s, I knew of him mostly through Diane Kessler, a member of the congregation I served as pastor from 1986-1995. When Jim Nash began his focused work on environmental ethics in the 1990s, I was a local pastor, and regrettably unable to keep pace with the burgeoning academic field of environmental ethics. Because of that, I am enormously grateful to Norm for his background paper on Nash's writings and reflections.

My contribution to tonight's conversation is not a look back, but a look forward. I've titled these comments: "Canary in a Coal Mine." They are a tribute to James Nash and the others I have named. The concerns, the warnings, the alarms which they began triggering four decades ago–those emergency strobe lights–are now all flashing. The reason is that in addition to all the important dimensions of environmental ethics that they lifted up, there is something new. We are the first generation to foresee, and the final generation with an opportunity to forestall, the most catastrophic effects of climate change. And our window to engage that opportunity is rapidly closing.

The significance of this reality cannot be overstated. Beginning with Aldo Leopold and Rachel Carson–or perhaps we should go back to Henry David Thoreau or even to Plato–environmental ethics has been concerned:

- with our relationship to the natural world,
- with our responsibility as stewards of God's creation,
- with issues of sharing, cooperation, distribution and victimization that all play-out in the arena of eco-justice,
- with the impact of various externalities on current and future generations, and
- with the interdependence and tension between personal interests and community interests

Each of these five points was brilliantly articulated in 1968 by Garrett Hardin in his article in *Science Magazine*, "The Tragedy of the Commons."[1]

Additionally, what scientific study has revealed over the last 20 years is an altogether different kind of issue. To the above concerns we must add something like Dale Aukerman's writing on nuclear war.[2] What is different, of course, is that nuclear war is a decision made by an elite few and carried out in a handful of seconds. Climate change is the result of the normal, daily behavior of the entirety of the human community carried out over a handful of generations. Both threaten to extinguish the life and beauty of the Eden into which we and our ancestors were born.

In a time such as this – and with only a few minutes at the microphone– what is the role of the church?

Simply put, it is impossible to contemplate the citizens, towns, corporations and countries of the world making the changes that are necessary unless they are inspired by transcendent motivations and led by religious leaders. We are all aware of numerous examples of how something like this has been done in the past, including the abolition of slavery, the end of child labor, the winning of the civil rights act, and the advancement of marriage equality and other GLBT concerns.

People of faith – not only Christians but people of every faith perspective–can base their engagement of the specific issue of Climate Change and the general issue of environmental degradation on two straightforward and universal theological principles.

First of all, our covenant with God is an everlasting covenant. Not only does God covenant with us, but God covenants with all future generations and with every living creature (Genesis 9:12). God's desire is that we – and untold generations of our descendants – have abundant life (John 10:10).

And the second principle is rooted in the most basic moral instruction of both the New Testament and Hebrew scriptures – a moral instruction found at the core of every world religion. We are called to love our neighbors as ourselves.

Over time, we have clarified our understanding of who our neighbor is. We have come to recognize that all people–regardless of the color of their skin, their class, their nationality, their sexual orientation–we have come to recognize that all people are our neighbors. Albert Schweitzer and others–including Jim Nash–have sought to expand our understanding of neighbor by setting aside our anthropocentric inclinations. They argue that all of life is sacred–not only the lives of humans.

Now it is essential that religious leaders further expand our understanding of neighbor so that the human community comes to accept that future generations are no less our neighbors than those who live next door to us today.

I believe this requires a re-purposing of the Church–a shift in our understanding of the vocation of the church–or what Jim Nash called "a Christian Ecological Reformation."

On a practical basis, what I mean is that within only 2 or 3 years, every 3rd or 4th sermon must touch upon the issues of Climate Change and the Environment. What I tell our 800 pastors and 392 churches is that if we don't make this shift, then in about 10-15 years every single sermon will focus on grief.

And in these frequent sermons they must advocate what I refer to as new "spiritual practices." We must adopt spiritual practices that involve changing the way we shop, eat, drive, share, spend, fly, use energy, recycle, and most importantly, engage as political advocates. Just as it is expected that religious people engage in daily prayer, we must make it part of our witness–part of our religious identity–to engage daily in lobbying for laws and international agreements that promote the commonwealth of all the world's living and yet-to-be born citizens and species.

After one read of "The Tragedy of the Commons" it becomes clear that international conferences or gatherings of global political and policy leaders such as those in Mexico City (2010) or earlier in Copenhagen (2009) require that religious or faith communities recognize their crucial role in global change. This encompasses at least two roles or responsibilities:

First: We must make our voices heard so that the laws and public policies that scientific research and analysis says must change will change. We might draw a lesson from the Civil Rights movement in the United States. The reason the people of Montgomery, Alabama, in 1956 undertook the spiritual practice of walking to work for 381 days was to change the laws of segregation.

Second: As the effects of climate change become more and more apparent, the unit of relevance and meaning will more and more become the town or other local political entity. I consider it something of a miracle that—as it turns out—there is a church in every town in the Commonwealth of Massachusetts and similar religious communities are located in almost every other political or geographic setting. If the church embraces the role to which God is calling it, I believe that the future is full of hope.

ENDNOTES
[1] Garrett, Hardin, "The Tragedy of the Commons," *Science*, vol. 162 (1968): 1243-1248
[2] Dale Aukerman, *Darkening Valley - A Biblical Perspective on Nuclear War* (New York: Seabury Press, 1981); see also: *Reckoning with Apocalypse - Terminal Politics and Christian Hope* (New York: Crossroad, 1993).

On James A. Nash, 'Loving Nature'

By Harvey Cox

The strongest feature of Jim Nash's book is that he is able to love nature with what might be called a "mature love," rather than an adolescent love, that is: without romanticizing it. In our earliest years we can "fall in love," and love people largely for what we project onto them, for what he would like them to be. As we mature we must "put away childish things," and love both people and things (and even ourselves) because God created them, because of who and what they *are*.

Just as I finished re-reading *Loving Nature*,[1] however, I bought a ticket, put on the 3-D glasses, and watched James Cameron's film, *Avatar*.[2] This film has been lauded by some as an environmentally friendly film. I found it just the opposite. Cameron's "nature" is nothing like the nature we find ourselves in and with. It is a glossy, hi-tech, enhanced version of nature. And it is a nature which the "Na'vi," the denizens of this post-modern nature do not need to love, cherish or care for. They are simply plugged into its throbbing universal network. On the other hand, the corporate-military enemies of this "neo-nature" are depicted as so brutal and malevolent it is impossible to see ourselves, and our often unconscious and even well intentioned destruction of nature, in their crushing onslaught. We meet "the enemy," but it is definitely not us. Cameron needs to "put away childish things," and show us real people in a real and really threatened nature, even if we see it through designer spectacles.

Nash's book also raises the difficult question of what we mean by intervention in nature, which he views with understandable suspicion. Where does "repairing the damage we have done," or "cleaning up our own mess," end and injurious intervention begin? Do we need a kind of "situational" environmental ethic? Jim Nash has raised, eloquently, all the right questions. Now the work he so well laid out begins.

ENDNOTES

[1] James Nash, *Loving Nature: Ecological Integrity and Christian Responsibility* (Nashville, TN: Abingdon Press, 1991).

[2] This epic science fiction film, *Avatar*, released in 2009, was written and directed by James Cameron. The film is set in 2154 when humans are mining a precious mineral on Pandora, a lush moon in the Alpha Centauri star system. The expansion of the mining colony threatens the continued existence of a local tribe, the Na'vi, a humanoid species indigenous to Pandora. The film's title refers to the genetically engineered hybrid bodies used by a team of researchers to interact with the natives of Pandora.

Summary of Discussion and Concluding Comments

By Norman Faramelli

There was lively discussion following the presentations. Many of those in attendance raised a variety of points and issues. We will note only of a few of them here.

The first comment was raised by panelist, John Hart in defense of the movie *Avatar*. Hart appreciated the theme of the movie—as a call for social and economic justice among the native Na'vi people to rise up against the corporate-military powers, who were concerned only with the materials they could extract from the ground. Some also raised the question about how this uprising took place. Others conceded that although the theme of exploited people might have some validity, the view of nature presented in *Avatar* was contrary to the understanding of nature found in the work of James Nash and other environmental ethicists. Nature was romanticized in the movie; Nash strongly opposed any attempt to romanticize nature. Also the juxtaposition of the innocent primitive Na'vi contrasted to the greedy, brutal mega machine of corporate/military power, can blind us to the reality that we are accomplices in the destruction of nature.

There were also several comments made about our intervention in the natural order. Intervention is not a new thing; it has occurred throughout history. In fact, many of the interventions are now needed to offset the negative consequences of previous interventions. We are not functioning in a pristine environment. It was clear that intervention always needs to be carried out with "humility," a virtue prominent in Nash's work.

On April 21, there were few of us who knew the extent of the Deepwater Horizon tragedy (that occurred on the previous day). We had not envisioned massive amounts of oil gushing into the Gulf of Mexico for months not just hours and days. Few of us could have contemplated how difficult it would be to stop the gushing oil and to seal the well. A deep humility is needed in the initial phase of any technological venture, because the "technical fix," to which we have become accustomed, might not be readily available. This was evident in the Deepwater Horizon disaster.

One of the most poignant comments raised was with regard Nash's last article, "The Bible versus Biodiversity: The Case Against the Moral Argument From Scripture." In this article, Nash played down the relevance of the direct application of Scriptural texts to contemporary situations. The question raised was: what will be the effects of this approach when we are trying to engage Evangelicals—who are deeply rooted in the Bible—in environmental causes? For instance, if we play down the importance of Scripture, do we not alienate our potential Evangelical allies? Although some noted that Nash might have just gotten tired of biblical proof-texting, others noted the title of the article itself. The article focused primarily on bio-diversity and Scripture. It is also clear that in Holy Scripture, the wilderness is not extolled for its magnificent flora and fauna, but it is a tough place where the religious and ethical commitments are tested under harsh circumstances.

It was also noted that even in this article, Nash demonstrated both a love and grasp of the biblical motifs. He was deeply familiar with the Bible, and studied it seriously. That is why in his last article; he does not throw out the Bible, but sees the necessity of the Bible engaging with other disciplines. Nash wrote:

The alternative method for Christian ethical evaluation, justification (or not) and prescription that I encourage is 'rational reflection on the fullness of human experience, in dialogue with the Bible and the Christian tradition, on the one hand, and cultural wisdom, especially in the relevant sciences and other religious, moral and philosophical traditions, on the others'. (See the Tribute to James Nash in this volume.)

As noted, there were many other points raised that evening that are not mentioned here. We continue to see the work of James Nash as critical in the development of the field of environmental ethics and ecological theology. We see his work in environmental ethics, environmental justice and eco-justice as pivotal to our understanding of current realities. Nash's insights serve as excellent points of departure for future work as noted by all of the panelists, especially the three doctoral students who will carry on that tradition. This utilization of Nash's work in environmental ethics is now happening. What I would also like to see is a fuller appreciation of James Nash as a theologian and ethicist of the ecumenical movement. As one ethicist told me, Nash's work in the Massachusetts area was not just a parochial effort, it was a critical element in the world-wide ecumenical movement, as Rodney Petersen noted in the Foreword to this volume.

Dealing with the issues of eco-justice and climate change cannot be done on a denominational level alone. It requires the participation of all Christian traditions, and so it needs to be fully ecumenical. But we need to take a step beyond that. This work cannot be done solely on a Christian plane alone—no matter how ecumenical. We need to find ways to engage all of the world religions, so this work needs to be fully interfaith, as well as ecumenical. But we even need to go beyond that. We need to engage not only people of faith, but also all people of good will—regardless of their theological or non-theological understanding. This is where Nash's understanding of ecological issues in light of the Natural Law tradition can be most helpful, especially as theology and ethics engage the social, physical and biological sciences.

We will always be indebted to James Nash for his energy, vision, creativity and his superb contributions to ecological ethics and to the ecumenical spirit. Above all, we are grateful to have been blessed by his presence and friendship.

Appendix I

By Norman Faramelli

*(Some Biographical Notes on James A. Nash,
first assembled by James A. Nash.)*

James A. Nash, of Burlington (Massachusetts), a social and ecological ethicist and self-described "church politician" died of leukemia on November 5, 2008. Born (1938) and reared in the newly unionized steel valley of western Pennsylvania. Nash was the proud son and grandson of Homestead and Duquesne steelworkers. He himself worked in the mills for short times. He lived in a low-income housing project on a bluff overlooking the orange-glowing mills along the biologically dead Monongahela River until he graduated from college, married and moved to Boston with his wife in 1960. These experiences deeply shaped his sense of social justice and ecological responsibility. Nash was a United Methodist elder who worked for the Massachusetts Council of Churches for twenty-one years (1967-1988).

Nash graduated from Grove City College (A. B. Magna cum laude,1960) and Boston University School of Theology (S.T. B. , magna cum laude, 1963). He received a Ph.D. in Social Ethics from Boston University in 1967, while a Rockefeller Doctoral Fellow in Religion (1965-67). He also studied ethics and politics at the London School of Economics (1963-64).

Nash's recreational passion was birding – along with camping, wildlife photography, and grueling hikes that the quest for birds often entailed of him. He was at home in a tent. He generally birded alone or with his wife (when death-march hikes were not involved). His favorite birding haunts included Big Bend, TX; Nome and Denali, AK; Southeastern AZ, and Plum Island, MA. Birding was an aesthetic and religious experience for him. The preservation of wildlife in wild places was one of his prime moral and political commitments.

Nash is survived by his beloved mentor, intimate friend, fellow frugalist and biking companion-his wife of 48 years, Millie as well as his loving family; daughters Noreen Nash of Cambridge, MA and Rebecca Nash of Gales Ferry, CT; granddaughter Haley Nash-Thompson of Gales Ferry, CT and brother, Norman Nash of Adrian, MI. These relationships confirmed his ultimate conviction:

Love is the ground and goal of being.

Appendix II

Selected Bibliography – The Works of James A. Nash

By Norman Faramelli

"Church Lobbying in the Federal Government: A Comparative Study of Four Church Agencies in Washington"; 1967—Ph.D. Dissertation—Boston University School of Theology.

Odyssey Toward Unity: Foundations and Functions of Ecumenism and Conciliarism, (Committee on purpose and Goals of Ecumenism, Massachusetts Council of Churches, 1978 (2nd printing). Nash was the principal author.

"Politically Feeble Churches and the Strategic Imperative," *The Christian Century*, vol. 99 (Oct. 6, 1982).

"Christian Liberalism: Ambiguous Legacy, Enduring Ethos," *The Unitarian Universalist Christian*.

"Political Conditions for Ecumenical Confession-A Protestant Contribution to the Emerging Dialogue," *Journal of Ecumenical Studies*, vol. 25, no. 2 (Spring 1988), pp. 241-261.

"From Mainline to Sideline: The Social Witness of the National Council of Churches," *Journal of Ecumenical Studies*, vol. 27, no. 4 (Fall 1990).

"The Logic of Solidarity: Commentaries on Pope John Paul II's Encyclical 'On Social Concern'," *Journal of Ecumenical Studies*, vol. 27, no. 4 (Fall 1990).

Loving Nature: Ecological Integrity and Christian Responsibility (Nashville, TN: Abington Press, 1991). Published in cooperation with the Churches Center on Theology and Public Policy.

"Ethical Concerns for the Global Warming Debate," *The Christian Century*, vol. 109, no. 25 (August 26, 1992).

"Human Rights and the Environment; New Challenge for Ethics," *Theology and Public Policy*, vol. 4, no. 2 (Fall 1992).

"Rio as a Political Event," *Theology and Public Policy* (Summer 1992).

"Biotic Rights and Human Ecological Responsibility," *The Annual of the Society of Christian Ethics*, 1993.

"What Does the Lord Require? How American Christians Think About Economic Justice," *Theology Today*, vol. 50, no. 3 (Oct. 1993).

"Case for Biotic Rights," *Yale Journal of International Law*, vol.18, no. 11 (1993), pp. 235-49.

"Ethics and the Economic-Ecology Dilemma: Toward a Just Sustainable and Frugal Future," *Theology and Public Policy*, vol. 6, no.1 (Summer 1994)

"On the Subversive Virtue: Frugality," in *Ethics of Consumption*, ed. D. Crocker and T. Linder (Rowan and Littlefield, 1997).

"AIDS, Gays and the American Catholic Church," *Commonweal*, vol. 122, no. 6 (March 24, 1995).

"A Response" to T. Derr's, "The Challenge of Biocentrism" in *Creation at Risk? Religion, Science and Environmentalism*, ed. M. Cromartie (Grand Rapids, MI: Eerdmans Publishing Co., 1995).

"On the Goodness of Government," *Theology and Public Policy*, vol. 7, no. 2 (1995), pp. 3-25.

"Toward the Revival and Reform of the Subversive Virtue: Frugality," *The Annual of the Society of Christian Ethics* (1995), pp. 137-160.

"Ecological Integrity and Christian Political Responsibility," *On Moral Business*, ed. Max Stackhouse (Grand Rapids, MI: Eerdmans Publishing Co., 1995).

"In Flagrant Dissent; An Environmentalist's Contention," in Thomas Derr (with James Nash and Richard Neuhaus) *Environmental Ethics and Christian Humanism* (Nashville, TN: Abington Press, 1996).

"Norms and the Man: A Tribute to Ian Barbour," *Bulletin of Science Technology and Society* (1996).

"Toward the Ecological Reformation of Christianity," *Interpretation*, vol. 50, no. 1 (Jan. 1996).

"Nature, Reality and the Sacred: The Nexus of Science and Religion," *Interpretation*, vol. 50, no. 1 (Jan. 1996).

"Moral Values in Risk Decisions," in *Handbook for Environmental Risk Decision Making: Values, Perceptions, and Ethics*, ed. C. Richard Cothern (Boca Raton, FL: CRC Press/ Lewis Publishers, 1996), pp. 199-200.

"The Politician's Moral Dilemma: Moral Responsibility and the Limits of Political Leadership Confronting the Ecological Crisis," *CTNS Bulletin* (Center for Theology and the Natural Sciences), vol. 16, no. 1 (Winter 1996), pp. 7-15.

"The Old Order Changeth: The Ecological Challenge to Christian Life and Thought," *Virginia Seminary Journal*, December 1997 (The Spriggs Lecture), pp. 6-11.

"Pulpit Politics: Faces of American Protestant Nationalism in the Twentieth Century," *Journal of the American Academy of Religion*, vol. 66, no. 3 (Fall 1998).

"Humility as Predisposition for Sustainability," *Bulletin of Science, Technology and Society*, vol. 19, no. 5 (October 1999), pp 359-364. (This was the 1999 Ian Barbour Lecture).

"Seeking Moral Norms in Nature: Natural Law and Ecological Responsibility," in *Christianity and Ecology: Seeking the Well-Being of the Earth and Humans*, eds. Dieter Hessel and Rosemary Radford Ruether (Cambridge, MA: Harvard University Press, 2000), pp 227-251.

"Healing an Ailing Alliance: Ethics and Science Face the Ambiguities in Water," *The Journal of Faith and Science Exchange* (Newton, MA: The Boston Theological Institute, 2001), pp. 111-123.

"Prodigality and Frugality: Core Conflict of the Times," in *Eco-Justice: The Unfinished Journey*, ed. William Gibson (Albany, NY: SUNY Press, 2004).

"Christianity, Contemporary," under Ecological Ethics in *The Encyclopedia of Religion and Nature*, ed. Bron Taylor (2005).

"Walter G. Muelder: Boston Personalism Incarnate," in *The Significance of Walter G. Muelder's Social Ethics Today: The Status of Personalism*, Boston Theological Institute, 2006.

"The Bible versus Biodiversity: The Case against Moral Argument from Scripture," in *The Journal for the Study of Religion, Nature and Culture*, vol. 3, no. 2 (2009).

In addition, Nash published numerous book reviews not noted here. He also wrote several key documents that he used for teaching purposes and gave many keynote addresses at various gatherings that were not published.

Contributors

The Rev. James Antal is Minster and President, Massachusetts Conference, United Church of Christ. He has been a major leader in the religious community in addressing ecological issues, especially those surrounding climate change.

The Rev. Dr. Harvey Cox is former Hollis Professor of Divinity, Harvard Divinity School and a noted author of numerous works. His "Secular City" played significant role in shaping the religious ethos in the 1960s. Cox is a Baptist minister. His most recent book is *The Future of Faith* (2010).

The Rev. Dr. Norman Faramelli is Lecturer in Philosophy, Theology and Ethics, Boston University School of Theology and an Adjunct in Christian Ethics at the Episcopal Divinity School. He is an Episcopal priest who has had a long history addressing eco-justice issues. He was a friend and colleague of Nash for over thirty years, and was also a participant in the Ethics and Sustainability Dialogue that Nash convened.

Ms. Tallessyn Grenfell-Lee is a doctoral student at the Boston University School of Theology who is focusing on ecological ethics and ecofeminism and its relationship to food production. She is an active member in the Methodist Church.

Dr John Hart is Professor of Christian Ethics, Boston University School of Theology. He is a Roman Catholic ethicist and highly regarded in ecumenical circles. Hart is the author of several notable books and articles. His most recent book is *Sacramental Commons: Christian Ecological Ethics* (2006).

Ms. Marla Marcum is a doctoral student at the Boston University School of Theology, who is on leave to be Coordinator of New England Climate Change Summer. She is Chair of, the Climate Change Task Force, New England Conference, United Methodist Church. She is also Director of Christian Education, Lexington United Methodist Church.

The Rev Shandirai Mawokamatanda is a doctoral student at the Boston University School of Theology focusing on peace, reconciliation and conflicts studies and their relevance to the situations in Africa. He is a Methodist minister.

The Rev. Dr. Rodney Petersen is Executive Director of the Boston Theological Institute. He has a long history in ecumenical activity including work with the World Council of Churches. He is the author of numerous books and articles, and the developer of Peace and Conflict studies in the BTI. On environmental ethics, his books include: *Consumption, Population, and Sustainability: Perspectives from Science and Religion* (2000) and *Earth at Risk: Advancing the Environmental Dialogue between Religion and Science* (2000).

The Rev. Dr. H. Paul Santmire is a theologian and former parish minister in the Lutheran Church. He previously served as Chaplain at Wellesley College. Santmire is the author of several pioneering works in the Theology of Ecology, such as *Brother Earth* (1970), *The Travail of Nature* (1985) and *Ritualizing Nature:. Renewing Christian Liturgy in a Time of Crisis* (2008).